NEW RULES

NEW RULES

Polite Musings from a Timid Observer

BILL MAHER

RODALE

Printed in the United States of America
Rodale Inc. makes every effort to use acid-free ∞, recycled paper ♻.

Book design by Christopher Rhoads
Cover photograph by Blake Little

Library of Congress Cataloging-in-Publication Data

Maher, Bill.
    New rules : polite musings from a timid observer / Bill Maher.
        p.   cm.
    ISBN-13 978-1-59486-505-3 paperback
    ISBN-10 1-59486-505-1 paperback
    1. American wit and humor.   I. Title.
PN6165.M34   2005
791.45'72—dc22   2005016222

Distributed to the book trade by Holtzbrinck Publishers

2   4   6   8   10   9   7   5   3   1   paperback

RODALE
LIVE YOUR WHOLE LIFE™

We inspire and enable people to improve their lives and the world around them
For more of our products visit rodalestore.com or call 800-848-4735

Acknowledgments

There are a lot of people to thank when a book comes out—the folks mentioned below are just the most prominent.

Lots of people thought a New Rules book would be a good idea, but Leigh Haber is the extraordinary editor who made it happen.

Michael Viner is the first name I think of when I think of books. He's doing the audio on this one, and any excuse to work with Mike is worth making.

Marc Gurvitz has been my manager forever and managed this book as well as he does everything. And thanks to Steve Lafferty at CAA, who got the ball rolling.

Polly Auritt of the *Real Time* staff did a great job getting the pictures we needed to help make you laugh.

And the writers of *Real Time*—Chris Kelly, Brian Jacobsmeyer, Ned Rice, Jay Jaroch, David Feldman, and Danny Vermont—are not just lol funny but know what time it is in America better than anyone I know.

Scott Carter, Sheila Griffiths, and Dean Johnsen produce *Real Time*, and their sensibility is unmistakably—thank goodness—on everything I do.

A very special thanks to HBO, especially Nancy Geller, for their unwavering support in providing me a forum to lay down these rules week after week.

And last, but really first, is my longtime producer/head writer of *Politically Incorrect*, and now *Real Time*, the Rob Petrie to my Alan Brady, Mr. Billy Martin. New Rules was his idea. I remember the fax he sent to me in 2002 as we were gearing up to launch a new show for HBO, borne of the ashes of *Politically Incorrect*, attemping to bring along what was good about that show and leave behind what we'd outgrown. Billy suggested New Rules as a segment, and I knew right away it was a keeper. Lucky for me, he has been as well.

And, corny as it may sound, I do cherish the bond between me and the audience, the minority that follows my stuff and always makes me glad it's us against the world.

Foreword

NEW RULE

No more books by talk show hosts! No, I mean it! Just this last one and then that's it. Who do we think we are, anyway?

I guess it's not enough to broadcast our every brilliant thought to millions of viewers each week. We also have to amass compilations of our favorite, most precious *bon mots* so that people can carry them around under their arms and enjoy them at the beach or on the subway or during a quiet moment sitting alone at home in a small room. Okay, okay, and they also make great gifts. There, I've said it.

But this book is different. It's not your typical, pompous fare where I, the all-knowing host, sit in judgment, presuming to know, through my vast experience as a media whore, how you should be living your lives. No, no— not at all. This is a simple, humble collection of rules that basically points out how everyone but me has their head up their ass. Trust me, it's a great read. And have I mentioned it also makes a great gift?

But here's why I really wanted to publish this book: whenever I'm at an airport waiting for a plane to take me to some stand-up gig, a stranger will invariably approach me and say, "Excuse me, sir, could you drop your pants so we can see what the dog is sniffing at?"

And that's why I wanted to make New Rules into a book—not just so there would be something else for people to discuss with me in airports, but also because it seemed about time that this "structureless" society of ours got back to the idea of rules, limits, and boundaries.

We have come to interpret the word "freedom" as meaning "without rules or boundaries," but that's not all there is to it. Kris Kristofferson wrote, "Freedom's just another word for nothing left to lose," apparently without considering that "nothing left to lose" is not another word at all, but four words. In doing so, he followed the rules of neither math nor grammar. What a loser.

And yet, when I was a teenager, I wanted to be just like Kris Kristofferson: grizzled. And not following the rules. Rules were for squares. I thought I was too cool for rules, which is quite amusing considering nothing about me at that age even remotely suggested coolness, except maybe my plaid polyester bell-bottoms. Of course, that's often the way it is: The urge to rebel in youth often predates having a reason to do so. But then one day you take a lawn dart in the kidney and suddenly following the rules—at least the rules about lawn darts—doesn't seem like such a bad idea.

I never did take a lawn dart in the kidney—that's just an example—but I did wake up one morning after a sleepover at John Waters's house to find my sleeping bag wasn't zipped up the same way as when I passed out. We all learn. It's just a matter of how and when.

Whatever happened to all of the rules we used to live by, anyway? Before the "Me" Generation, followed by the "Me, Me, Me" Generation, followed by the "What Part of Me Don't You Understand?" Generation, there were rules—rules like "No trespassing," "No shoes, no shirt, no service," and "Please don't touch the dancers"—and they applied to everyone. Nowadays, these same rules are either ignored completely or viewed more as suggestions to be followed á la carte, depending on which ones we like.

And our respect for rules seems to be fluid, depending on convenience. Take "Do not feed the ducks." That rule would seem easy enough to follow, especially if we have no intention of feeding the ducks in the first place. But if we've come all this way with a carload of toddlers and a sack full of bread, what's a little duck feeding going to hurt? It is presumptions like that one, that rules apply more to others than to ourselves, that have placed society into disarray and Martha Stewart into an electronic ankle bracelet.

Even our trusted leaders can't be counted on to observe the rules—or at least they do so only selectively. "Rule of law!" Remember that popular refrain from the days of the Clinton impeachment? As House Republicans told us at the time, they really had no choice. It was all out of their hands. Legislators are bound to uphold the rules as they're written, no matter what—except, apparently, as they apply to subpoenaing the brain dead. And by "the brain dead," of course, I mean baseball's Mark McGwire.

Rules are the signposts that define where our rights end and those of our fellow citizens begin. Adhering to rules and abiding by a code of civility—this is what separates us from the apes . . . and Tom DeLay. Stop following the rules and you start stepping on toes. And that's where this book comes in—not necessarily to rehash our old, out-of-date rules but to establish new ones for a self-obsessed, success-by-any-means, get-mine culture. These are the rules that, frankly, were not necessary back when we practiced those old-fashioned time wasters: courtesy, consideration, and common sense.

Rules are important—we all need them. They provide structure and help us to know where we stand with others. That's why I'm constantly fighting with my neighbors—no rules. Okay, and because the makeup sex is fantastic. When we disregard the rules altogether we get anarchy or, worse yet, Enron.

Of course, children need structure and rules, too. I've always said the three most important things for a child to learn are respect, accountability, and to shut the hell up on airplanes. Rules help shape kids and let them know that they're loved. Children not subject to these healthy boundaries often find themselves, by the time they are teenagers, lacking any real sense of security or self. These kids are destined, sadly, for social difficulties, school shootings, or, even more likely, session after session of red-hot car sex with their French teacher.

Children, though, who are exposed to the healthy, enforced rules of conscientious parenting seem to grow to their "right size," complete with a moral compass. There is no limit to how far a child can go with just a little discipline and structure. Just look at what the Hitler Youth did for the pope.

So, then, here you have them—my New Rules for a better world, for all of you out there who love freedom but still crave a little structure. This book, come to think of it, is a lot like having to drop your pants at the airport: There's an important point to it, but mostly it's just plain funny. So, enjoy it! And did I mention, it also makes a great gift?

BILL MAHER

NEW RULES

A Perfect Cliché

NEW RULE

Stop calling it a "perfect storm" when two bad things happen at the same time. Sometimes it's just some crap happening at the same time as some other crap. Let's go back to what we used to call it before that movie about George Clooney and his epic struggle to kill more tuna: Shit happens.

AND NEW RULE

I don't care that your phone takes pictures. It's a phone, not a Swiss Army knife. Great, now the annoying camera buff and the annoying cell phone prick can merge as one guy. Hey, if you can figure out how to make that "camera phone" play country-western music real loud, we could call it "a perfect storm of assholes."

A Suit and Battery

NEW RULE

Now that you've won and you're safe, you have to tell us: What the hell was that thing on your back during the debate?

AARP Yours

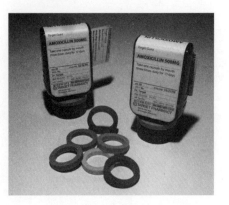

NEW RULE

Stop fucking with old people. Target is introducing a redesigned pill bottle—it's square, with a bigger label, and the top is now the bottom. And by the time Grandpa figures out how to open it, his ass will be in the morgue. Congratulations, Target, you've just solved the Social Security crisis.

Abigail Van Buried

NEW RULE

Dead people can't write advice columns. Dear Abby has been dead for years, yet she continues her daily syndicated column. If I want to hear what a corpse thinks, I'll read Robert Novak.

Abu Grab-Ass

NEW RULE

Lynndie England and Charles Graner should not be sentenced to jail. They should be photographed performing sex acts, stacked in a pile of naked people, and stripped of their dignity. Or as it's better known here, *The Real World*.

Accessories after the Fact

NEW RULE

Martha Stewart does not need an electronic ankle bracelet. There's a caravan of news vans on her driveway, choppers overhead, and paparazzi with telephoto lenses in the trees—where the hell is she gonna go? Plus, what sense does it make to remand a "home diva" to her home? That's like sentencing Kirstie Alley to check in nightly at IHOP.

Ad-Nauseum

NEW RULE

Stop running TV ads I don't understand. I'm not sure if IBM's latest is advertising weapons of mass destruction or stool softener. Then there's the one with clouds moving in fast motion, some Buddhist monks on a cell phone, and James Earl Jones saying, "We're the world leader in virtual network upstream data retrieval." What?! Hey, fuck you. I watch TV to see bimbos marry strangers for money. If I want to be confused, I'll take mushrooms.

Alter, Boys

NEW RULE

The Catholic Church needs to change its name to Tollhouse Cookies. A new study reveals the tally of Catholic priests who've been accused of molestation in the United States is approaching 5,000, which means it's time to change the name and start over. That's what Phillip Morris did when their name became synonymous with lung cancer—they became the good people at the Altria company. Kentucky Fried Chicken wanted you to forget the "fried" part and became KFC. So how 'bout it, Roman Catholic Church—or should I say "RCC"?

Anchors Away

NEW RULE

Stop calling the media "elite" and "liberal" and start calling it what it really is—lazy. It came out recently that the Bush administration has been producing its own "news" segments, complete with their own "correspondents," and sending them off to local news outlets who aired them untouched. No wonder Hunter Thompson blew his brains out. I'm sorry, but the local news is not the place for government propaganda; it's the place for car chases, kittens caught in trees, and a "meteorologist" whose previous job was at Hooters.

Aromatic Transmission

NEW RULE

No, we don't need a Hummer cologne. Yes, Hummer is now also a men's fragrance. They say the scent is a masculine combination of leather, sandalwood, and a bald man's tiny cock. It's also great cologne for gay guys: You put it on and, before you know it, you're rolling over.

Ash Hole

NEW RULE

Mount St. Helens has to either blow up or shut up. We get it—you're America's celebrity volcano. I say we kill two divas with one stone, and the next time Mount St. Helens starts to blow, we throw Paris Hilton in it.

To Surrogate with Love

NEW RULE

To all the conservative women out there: If you're so sure the embryos needed for stem cell research are precious human life that can't be destroyed, then implant one in your uterus and bring it to term. That's right, put your cervix where your mouth is.

Right now in America, there are thousands of stem cells sitting in fertility clinics that are not allowed to be used for research, *will be* destroyed after a year or two, and could be right now implanted in a lady's hoo-hoo to make a screaming, mewling infant that would ironically make you sorry *you* were ever born.

Here's how far back along the chain of life stem cells are: They're called stem cells because they haven't even decided what kind of cells they're going to be, so it's very close to declaring that life begins when you're just thinking about fucking somebody. Which is just about how most right-wing prudes like George Bush would like it. This is, after all, an administration that absolutely hates Planned Parenthood—but then again, judging by Iraq, they hate planned anything.

Did you know that our president spent the entire month before 9/11 on his ranch, working on the stem cell issue, trying, as he said, to bridge the worlds of ethics and science? Seriously, could there be anything George Bush knows less about than ethics and science?

Here's something that may be life: a tiny speck of subatomic goo. Here's something that *is* life: Michael J. Fox. One is invisible to the naked eye, the other was in *Back to the Future*.

With stem cell research properly funded, scientists believe we could do everything from curing Parkinson's to regenerating spinal cord tissue in Democrats.

So, ladies of the right, what do you say? There are thousands of extra embryos sitting around in fertility clinic freezers all over America right now, just waiting for a good home. So if you're not gonna finish those eggs, come on, go ahead, knock yourself up.

BILL MAHER

NEW RULES

Bad & Plenty

NEW RULE

You can't call it a treat if everyone hates it. We toppled Saddam Hussein—why can't we get rid of candy corn? Anyone who hands this stuff out on Halloween hates your children and wants them to die; they just don't have the guts to stick a razor blade in an apple.

Bargain Bins

NEW RULE

No, it's not okay if you buy my coffin at Costco. That's right, Costco is now selling reasonably priced caskets—aisle seven, between the Metamucil and the adult diapers. But in doing so, they're depriving us of one of the most critical stages of the grieving process—getting screwed out of four grand by a sleazy funeral home director. Plus, making your kids pay through the nose when you die is often the only payback for that "tuition" money they spent on beer.

Bawl Game

NEW RULE

Stop wallowing. Several years after 9/11, ballparks still insist on a giant seventh inning buzzkill with a somber rendition of "God Bless America." There's a thin line between loving America and stalking it. Please, we've already sung the national anthem. Now let me honor America the right way: by getting drunk on overpriced beer and yelling obscenities at millionaires on steroids.

Be Real

NEW RULE

Call things what they are. If your morning coffee contains crushed ice, whipped cream, and caramel, it's a milk shake. Same as if you cook your cocaine on a spoon and smoke it, you're not freebasing; you're a crackhead. And if you go down on your husband after he gives you a new fur coat, you're not celebrating your anniversary; you're a—oh, never mind.

Bear Ass

NEW RULE

Don't try to get pandas to mate by showing them porn. Yes, the Chinese government is really doing that. But it's not working because after watching all that porn, the male pandas keep pulling out and coming on her teats.

Biker Chic

NEW RULE

Cheering for Lance Armstrong doesn't make you an international cycling aficionado. Unless you can name one other rider in the Tour de France in the last 100 years, you're not a fan. You're just someone who likes it when America beats foreigners. And by the way . . .

. . . you're also not a tennis expert if you like watching Russian teenagers bounce up and down. You're just a perv.

Blow Hard III: Blow Harder!

NEW RULE

When actors volunteer for war, take them. In a gesture of immense empti-ness, Bruce Willis called President Bush and offered to go fight in Iraq. President Bush told him it was unlikely to happen, but they'd get back to him if they couldn't get Vin Diesel.

Body Shop

NEW RULE

Family members get to sell their dead loved ones. After the UCLA med-ical school was found to be selling cadavers for profit, a scandal erupted. But shouldn't families be allowed to do this directly? Those nursing homes aren't free, you know. Now that Grandma's dead, it's about time she started pulling her weight. If you just parted her out like an old Honda Civic, the cost of abandoning her all these years to the care of minority health care workers bent on racial payback would be recouped over time.

Booze Clues

NEW RULE

You don't need to study malt liquor. A groundbreaking study found that malt liquor usually comes in a bigger bottle, has more alcohol than regular beer, and is largely a drink of the homeless and unemployed—all facts most people learn after their first date with Tara Reid. Let me save you guys some time: Jägermeister and Mad Dog 20/20 aren't varieties of Pinot, either.

Bore Play

NEW RULE

Cuddling is for girls. The latest rage in New York is "cuddle parties," where grown men and women put on pajamas and just . . . cuddle. Pardon me while I throw up. Participants say it's not about sex; it's about intimacy. No, it's about sex. You're just so neurotic and emasculated that you've decided to skip the screwing entirely and go right to the boring part afterward. The only time a man should say "I need a hug" is if he's choking.

Bored of the Rings

NEW RULE

Three and a half hours is too long for a movie about magical midgets. *The Lord of the Rings: The Return of the King* is so long, you have to take a pee break before you get through the title. The *Rings* trilogy runs almost nine hours. If I want to spend that kind of time seeing dragons, I'll take drugs.

Brag Bashing

I don't care how fast your kid read the last *Harry Potter*. That doesn't make him gifted. This kid is gifted . . .

. . . and the only thing he's ever read is a home pregnancy test.

Brew Ha Ha

If you can't get drunk at a fraternity, it's not a fraternity. It's a club. UC Berkeley has banned alcohol at fraternity parties, which is sort of like banning black people on *Soul Train*. You can't make frat guys stay sober. Then they'll see all their late-night streaking, fanny paddling, and tea bagging for what it really is—Delta Kappa Gay.

Bulletin Bored

NEW RULE

We don't need a FOX "News Alert" every time something explodes in Iraq. It's a war—breaking news would be when stuff *stops* blowing up. Until then, we'll assume Baghdad is just like Lindsay Lohan—getting bombed daily.

Bush Whack

NEW RULE

George Bush must stop saying he owes all his success to Laura. George Bush owes all his success to his daddy, his daddy's friends, trust funds, legacy admissions, the National Guard, the Supreme Court, Karl Rove, Dick Cheney, and AA.

But Siriusly

NEW RULE

Paying to listen to the radio is wrong. Seemingly normal Americans are now paying 10 dollars a month to get satellite radio. That's right—they're paying to listen to the radio. Hello! It's the radio! The whole point of radio is that you don't have to pay for it. It's like paying to hum. If it wasn't free, do you think they'd play Foghat? So what if satellite radio has a hundred channels. So does cable TV, and just like cable TV, 5 of them are good, 20 suck, and the rest are in Spanish.

Butt Out

NEW RULE

Sodomy rules! If it's still asking too much to legalize the blow job, let's start with medicinal blow jobs and work from there. What two consenting adults choose to do in the privacy of a casting office is their business.

Byte Me

NEW RULE

Computers aren't for voting; they're for picking up underage girls. Voting by computer sounds really cool and futuristic—if this were 1969. But now that we all have computers, we know that they are, in fact, huge fuck-up machines. They're like having a compact, silicon version of Gary Busey on your desk—you never know what's going to happen. I'll tell you what'll happen: Some 13-year-old hacker in Finland is going to hand the presidency to Kylie Minogue. You thought the 2004 election was bad—wait until the next one is decided by a customer service rep in New Delhi.

Truth in Labeling

NEW RULE

Stop believing slogans, especially the ones that come out of the White House. Twinkies aren't wholesome goodness, and the "Clear Skies Initiative" isn't really going to bring clear skies. And it turns out that the "No Child Left Behind" law actually leaves lots of children behind. It leaves so many behind, in fact, that they have a name for them now: "pushouts," as in "we're pushing you out of school so that our cumulative test scores will be higher."

Yes, that's what this is all about. Our "No Child Left Behind" law is written like this: As a state, you get federal money for your schools, but only when two main things happen—you make test scores go up and dropout rates go down. How best to achieve both of those goals? By making the dumber kids . . . disappear!

The "Texas Miracle" in education, it turns out, was all about raising test scores by making almost the entire bottom half of the class drop out, and then falsely lowering the dropout rate by putting those students in phony categories like "transferred" or "enrolled in GED" or "dating Demi Moore."

We weren't actually improving the system, but we were making it look like we were where it matters: on paper. It's not for nothing that all those Texans looked up to Enron. For the 2000 election, Houston's dropout rate was given as 1.5 percent. After the election, it was revised to *40 percent*, probably by the same guy who makes up the budget. I don't need a degree in fuzzy math to know that 40 percent is not "no child left behind."

And if you say "no child" in your law, it takes a Texas-size nerve to then treat those kids like cards in a gin rummy game, where you get to ditch the two low ones, and where bodies just disappear like dissidents in Argentina or that Heather Locklear airport drama.

George Bush ran for office as the education guy, and his caring about leaving no child behind is what softened him into a compassionate conservative. So it seems wrong to find out that what we're really doing is just handing lots of kids a GED kit and telling them, "Good luck exploring your other educational opportunities, like learning how many vials of crack you can carry in your underwear."

As no one could tell you better than our president himself, we don't all blossom early in life, so maybe writing off so many kids so early isn't so wise. It might amuse the President to know that this is exactly what they do in his favorite country, France, but France has more of a social safety net than we do. Our safety net has a name. It's called prison.

People say education is the cornerstone of our democracy—they're wrong, of course. The cornerstone of our democracy is campaign cash and lots of it. But shouldn't education still count for something? As the president himself might say, "We can do gooder."

BILL MAHER

NEW RULES

C3 Pee-Yew

NEW RULE

You can stop releasing *Star Wars* now. We've seen it. I don't care if it's in a box set, if it's remastered or redigitized, if there are bonus scenes or a director's commentary; it's still a space movie for guys who can't get laid.

Call Hating

NEW RULE

Ass-kissing must be done in person. Yes, I'll "continue to hold" but not because you said, "Your call is important to us." If my call was really important to you, you'd hire a human to pick up the damn phone.

Can You Hear Me Now?

NEW RULE

No more cell phones in movie theaters. You're not a cardiologist on call—you're a putz whose babysitter wants to know where the ketchup is. And then you tell her, in the middle of the movie! Sometimes it's so loud in the theater, I can barely hear what the black people are yelling at the screen. There's a simple solution: Put your cell phone on vibrate and then up your ass.

Car Tune Network

NEW RULE

Keep your homemade mix CDs to yourself. I know you spent weeks trying to pick the perfect song to put between "Hey Ya" and "Who Let the Dogs Out," but I don't even like music. I only wear an iPod to avoid talking to you.

Cell Lout

NEW RULE

Don't call me when you're stuck in traffic. It's not my fault radio sucks. And did it ever occur to you that there wouldn't be so much traffic if people like you put down the phone and concentrated on the road? Besides, I can't talk now—I'm in the car behind you, trying to watch a DVD.

Center Old

NEW RULE

Just because you used to be famous doesn't mean you belong in *Playboy*. A recent issue features a photo spread with Debbie Gibson, perfectly nice woman, whose "electric youth" ended in 1988. Here's a way to tell if you're an '80s icon who shouldn't be naked: When you sit down, your "leg warmers" are your tits. If I want to be exposed to has-been pop stars, I'll sleep over at Neverland.

Check Your Local Lispings

NEW RULE

Enough with "gay-sploitation" TV. *Queer Eye for the Straight Guy?* If I want a bunch of gay men in queeny outfits telling me how to live my life, I'll go back to MASS.

Checkout Whine

NEW RULE

I'm not the cashier! By the time I look up from sliding my card, entering my PIN number, pressing "Enter," verifying the amount, deciding, "No, I don't want cash back," and pressing "Enter" again, the kid who's supposed to be ringing me up is standing there eating my Almond Joy. Paper? Plastic? I don't have time for that! I've just been called to do cleanup on aisle nine.

Chief Wannabe

NEW RULE

If you have to tell me what fraction of you is Native American, you're not really an Indian. There's a word for people who claim to be one-quarter Indian: Puerto Rican.

Chock Full o' Putz

NEW RULE

The more complicated the Starbucks order, the bigger the asshole. If you walk into a Starbucks and order a decaf grande half-soy half-low-fat iced-vanilla double-shot gingerbread cappuccino extra dry light ice with one Sweet'N Low and one NutraSweet . . . you're a huge asshole. If you're this much of a control freak about coffee, you must be really unbearable when it comes to something important, like a Danish.

Chopping Spree

NEW RULE

If you don't want the world to think your religion is medieval, stop beheading people. Texans are bloodthirsty and dim, and even they learned to use an electric chair. Come on, Islam. Join the nineteenth century.

LAX Security

NEW RULE

Homeland Security can't call itself Homeland Security until it provides homeland security.

According to an FBI report, airlines are still a prime target for al-Qaeda, mainly because airline security in America remains a faith-based initiative. President Bush has certainly proved himself resolute when he wants to make something an issue—so we really could use his steely resolve on this one. Or, to paraphrase Judge Judy, "Don't pee on my leg and tell me you're a bomb-sniffing dog."

As a comedian, I do a lot of flying, and some of it is in airplanes, which unfortunately only leave from airports, which have become bureaucratic nightmares that test our patience, our sense of logic, and our ability to hide a small brick of hash inside a hollowed-out can of deodorant.

If you're looking for a reason terrorists haven't hijacked another plane, I think I know what it is: It's too much of a hassle! I mean seriously, people, I'm on the road a lot—sometimes I honestly can't remember who packed my bag!

Did you hear the latest? Now there can be no lighters on planes. This, of course, will do nothing to change the safety equation, but it will ensure that

Class-Holes

Stop giving me that pop-up ad for Classmates.com. There's a reason you don't talk to people for 25 years—because you don't particularly like them. Besides, I already know what the captain of the football team is doing these days—mowing my lawn.

if the passengers end up enjoying the terrorists' work, they still can't bring them back for an encore.

And the new luggage screening system, which everyone agrees would help a lot, remains on the drawing board because the Bush administration insists the airlines should pay for it. Are they high? The airlines are broker than Michael Jackson. Delta announced last week it was taking away the pillows—*the pillows?* That's like Holiday Inn saying they can't afford the mint. Plus, now what am I supposed to use to muffle the crying kid next to me?

There's what we pay lip service to, and then there's what we pay money for, which is, after all, what we actually "value." We could have good security at the airport; we know how to do it. Have you ever been to a casino? There are more cameras than at a Korean wedding, with zoom lenses that can count the stitches on your date's sex change from 50 feet away. You can't do math in your head in a casino without being spotted, recorded on videotape, hustled off the floor, and buried in the desert by Joe Pesci.

So what I'm saying is, Am I just a dreamer, or could we try to make the airports at least as secure as Circus Circus?

Closed-Mouth Session

NEW RULE

Congressional sing-alongs of "God Bless America" are the cheapest form of political pandering. We get it. You're on our side. Now get back to work. Those lobbyists in your office aren't going to blow themselves.

Color Scheme

NEW RULE

Color-coded terror alerts are not just for campaigns. I can't remember the last time we had one. It must have been . . . anytime John Kerry tried to speak. Okay, the terror alerts stopped the same second as the election, but that doesn't mean they were fake. That's just being paranoid. If you think Bush would do something like that, you might as well say he hires fake reporters, bribes columnists, and produces his own news.

Coming-Out Party

NEW RULE

If your father is a dangerous zealot who describes homosexuals as "sinners" who practice "selfish hedonism," you have a moral duty to become a lesbian. Congratulations to Alan Keyes's daughter Maya, who did just that. Now, if you can just get yourself impregnated by David Crosby and then immediately get an abortion, I think we can drive Daddy right over the edge.

Coming Too Soon

NEW RULE

Stop bringing out DVDs so soon. I'm still ignoring you in the theater.

Corntroversy

NEW RULE

Cornbread isn't bread. It's cake.

Coronary Eatery

NEW RULE

Your hamburger can't be bigger than your ass. Denny's Beer Barrel Pub in Clearfield, Pennsylvania, is offering a new burger that weighs 15 pounds. One sign your portions may be too large: if one of the health risks is a back injury.

Crappy Meal

NEW RULE

You can't put any more types of meat on a bacon cheeseburger. Once you've made it a bacon cheeseburger, you're done. If you're adding more than that, you have to opt out of Medicare.

Prescriptures

NEW RULE

Pharmacists have to fill prescriptions. More and more American pharmacists are refusing to fill prescriptions for birth control because of their personal moral objections. You know what would really teach us a lesson? If you took off your pretend doctor jacket and got another job.

Or maybe I'm wrong. Maybe cutting off the Pill doesn't go far enough. It's high time activist drugstores stopped coddling sluts in every aisle. Let's not sell any more makeup, either. A good woman doesn't paint herself. And no more deodorant. You should smell bad—keeps the boys from getting ideas. And no suntan lotion—I've seen what happens at the MTV beachhouse, you whore. You want to avoid melanoma, buy a veil.

Why is this country becoming Utah? I know the conservatives are always saying that the coastal elites don't really "get it" about them because we just "fly over." Okay, maybe, but you guys don't get us either: We need sex. Refusal to provide birth control threatens our economy and our very way of life here in Southern California. There's a lotta hot chicks out here, man; we need birth control. Seriously—I mean, how do you think movies get made?

Now, of course, I know the other side is saying, yes, but this is a moral issue. Problem is, not everyone gets their morals from the same book. You go by the book that says slavery is okay but sex is wrong—until after marriage, at which point it becomes a blessed sacrament between a husband and the wife who's withholding it.

In conclusion, let me say to all the activist pharmacists out there, the ones who think sex is bad, probably because sex with them always is: A pharmacist is not a lawmaker, or even a doctor—in the medical pecking order, you rank somewhere in between a chiropractor and a tree surgeon. You don't answer to a law higher than the laws of men. You work for Save-On. The doctors are the ones who make the medical decisions because they're the ones who went to medical school, whereas you were just transferred from the counter where people drop off film.

BILL MAHER

NEW RULES

Defense Mechanism

NEW RULE

Lay off Rumsfeld and his 9/11 memento. Yes, Donald Rumsfeld took a piece of the airplane that hit the Pentagon—like you've never lifted anything from work. But he kept it for a good reason: to remind himself of who did this to us. Otherwise, we might have retaliated against the wrong country.

Déjà View

NEW RULE

Enough with the reunion shows. First we endured *Dallas* getting back together, then the gang from *Happy Days*. That didn't make me say, "I wonder what Schneider's been up to?" If I cared about what a bunch of has-beens from the '80s thought, I'd have backed Bush's war plans.

Deliverance

Britney Spears and her husband have to name their new baby "Shithead." It's the redneck version of "Apple." And while we're at it, stop bugging her about smoking—it's a little late to start worrying about the DNA when half of it is Kevin Federline's.

Devout of His Mind

NEW RULE

Pat Robertson is insane. Just because he smiles and wears a nice suit doesn't mean he's any less of a whack job than all those wild-eyed, urine-stained nut bags who babble on street corners about Jesus through a bullhorn. And he's getting desperate, because after you've agreed that the purple Teletubby is gay, where do you go? It's like Madonna when she needs attention. She has to keep upping the ante. In a year or two, she'll have nothing left to do but anal. And by then, no one will care. Except Pat Robertson.

Diet-Netics

NEW RULE

Scientology makes you fat. John Travolta, Kirstie Alley, Lisa Marie Presley: fat, fat, fat! L. Ron Hubbard went to the cupboard to fetch his old dog a bone. But it was gone, because his followers scarfed it. Be honest: It's not a religion; it's just an excuse for a bake sale.

Don't Be Hatin'

NEW RULE

You can't criticize a governor for not hiring black people for his cabinet when his state has no black people. No, when he was governor of Vermont, Howard Dean never appointed an African-American to his cabinet, possibly because there's only one African-American in Vermont, and she's on the maple syrup bottle.

Don't Go Greek

NEW RULE

No gay fraternities. Apparently, there are now dozens of them. Why bother? If you're gay, you already have a much better way of bonding with another man than the chug-a-lug. Fraternities are for fucking assholes, not for fucking assholes.

Don't Play It Again, Sam

NEW RULE

Everyone has to stop pretending Woody Allen movies don't completely suck. Hollywood stars must stop pretending that it's an honor to appear in his unwatchable, recycled tripe, and critics have to stop pretending that a tiny old Jew could be scoring with Tea Leoni and Helen Hunt. Somebody contact wardrobe—the emperor has no clothes.

Du Jour Job

NEW RULE

Room service personnel must know what the soup is! You're working the phones at room service. What do you think you're going to get asked—what you're wearing? If I'm paying 28 dollars for two eggs and a Coke, you should know the soup, all the state capitals, and where I left my keys.

Not Another Teen Movie

NEW RULE

Somebody make a movie I want to go see. If you're asking why movies have gotten so bad, I'll tell you why: It's because Hollywood studios now get 60 percent of their money from DVDs, all of which are bought by the young, dumb male demographic, the same one that's given us *Maxim* magazine, attention deficit disorder, and George Bush.

When I was a teenager, Hollywood didn't give a damn about me—and that was good! Good for the movies and good for me because I was challenged—to smarten up instead of dumbing down. Besides ruining movies, we've also managed to ruin our kids by making everything be about them. And now if I want to see a movie, I had better like loud noises, things blowing up, and Colin Farrell.

Movies suck because Hollywood has figured out that Mom and Dad don't spend their money on movies anymore; they give their money to their kids and *they* spend it on movies—to break up their shopping sprees at the mall. It's like American parents are on one long date with their kids—no, it's even worse; it's like Robert DeNiro in *Casino*, helplessly trying to buy the love of a shopaholic hooker with no heart, played, of course, by Sharon Stone.

Before I die, could someone please make one more movie I want to go see? I'm not asking for the moon here, and I'm not some film snob with a ponytail who only likes subtitled Albanian documentaries. But to middle-aged people like me, a good movie is like good sex—you don't have to put one out every day, but when whole seasons go by without getting one, you do start to get a little horny for entertainment.

BILL MAHER

NEW RULES

Eddie Iz

NEW RULE

Transvestites are gay. I know what you're going to say: "Bill, not all transvestites are gay." Yes, they are. Studies show . . . aw, screw studies. Yes, they are.

Elimistate

NEW RULE

The next reality show must be called *America's Stupidest State*. We'll start at 50, and each week, if your state does something really stupid with, say, evolution or images of the Virgin Mary, you'll move on to the next round. Of course, the final five will always end up being Alabama, Utah, Kansas, Texas, and Florida. Sorry, Tennessee.

Emerald Ale

NEW RULE

This St. Patrick's Day—if you want to get drunk, just get drunk. Don't blame Ireland. Why is the drunk the only Irish icon we celebrate on March 17? What about the unreadable novelist, the unwatchable playwright, the unbearable clog dancer? Or the fat cop, the crooked mayor, the shifty bomber, the incompetent waitress, the fiery spinster schoolmarm, the dowdy upstairs maid, and the sadistic lesbian nun?

Emission Impossible

NEW RULE

Dating a self-proclaimed 26-year-old virgin is probably not the best way to stifle the gay rumors. You're a big star, you can have any woman you want, and you pick the one actress in town who doesn't put out? I thought Scientology was supposed to *clear* your mind.

Entertainment Weakly

NEW RULE

No more TV gambling. First, there was *Celebrity Poker*, then there was *Celebrity Blackjack*. I saw one show that was just Camryn Manheim scratching lottery tickets. What gets on TV has to be at least as interesting as what's on the average security monitor at a convenience store.

Exit Pole

NEW RULE

Don't lop off your boyfriend's penis and flush it down the toilet. That's what Kim Tran of Anchorage, Alaska, did recently after she and her boyfriend had a spat: She cut off his penis and flushed it down the toilet. Whatever happened to the silent treatment?

Exit, Poll

NEW RULE

Stop taking stupid polls. Every little news program on every cable news network has their own dumb-ass online poll. And it's always some ridiculous question like, "We want to know what you think. Is John Bolton too much of an asshole, not enough of an asshole, or just the right amount of asshole?" This is America. Knowing nothing and choosing one of two options isn't a poll. It's an election.

Assisted Leaving

NEW RULE

Just because you have a job for life doesn't mean you have to do it for life. It's well and proper that we venerate our elders—but give it a freakin' rest. To every thing, there is a season. Turn! Turn! Turn! A time to reap, a time to sow. And a time to pack it in, put on a housecoat, and fall asleep in front of the Golf Channel.

Now, I know it must be hard to give up your job when your job is literally sitting on a throne, or being on a "supreme" court, or keeping women out of your priesthood to make room for the gays—but at some point it starts to look like you think of yourself as indispensable, and no one is indispensable, including you, the late Mr. Infallible. I don't want to say the pope was out of it, but at the end he was caught saying two Our Fathers and three *Proud Marys*.

And Queen Elizabeth, your son has been waiting so long to be king, even his mistress is a senior citizen. Queen for 50-plus years, it's a good run—second only to *Cats*. But now it's time to kick off those royal slippers, smell the English roses, and spend some time with those Nazi grandkids.

I don't understand America. We work until we have strokes, then after we die, our estates are fought over, and we're turned into Soylent Green and eaten.

You know who knows how to live? Titans of industry: Ray Kroc, Colonel Sanders, Dave from Wendy's—none of them spent their golden years tied to a desk. They all died of heart disease from eating their own food.

In conclusion, there's a reason that names like Cary Grant, Joe DiMaggio, and Johnny Carson inspire a special kind of awe: They all did something that made them more beloved than anyone else—they left before we got sick of them. They didn't make us all pretend to yawn to get them to leave the party. They looked around, as all of us will someday, and said, I've done my part, I've said my piece, and I'm finally deaf enough to stand being home all day with my spouse.

BILL MAHER

NEW RULES

Face Reality

NEW RULE

Stop being shocked when reality TV contestants turn out to be wife beaters, drug addicts, shoplifters, and porn stars. They're letting us marry them to strangers and make them eat eel shit. They don't have the gene for shame—that's why they're on reality shows.

Faking the Band

NEW RULE

No playing guitar and harmonica at the same time. Yes, I know it's possible, but it always sounds like shit, and you look like an idiot doing it. If you must have both playing at the same time, hire another musician. How much can a harmonica player cost? Wearing a harmonica harness is only acceptable if you make a living performing in the subway, and you have cymbals strapped to your knees.

Fantastic Bore

NEW RULE

Let's make at least every second American movie not based on a comic book. How many of you knew the film *Sideways* was actually based on a comic book called *The Tedious Adventures of Drunk Man and Horny*? If we keep making superhero movies, the rest of the world is going to start seeing America as some kind of infantile fantasyland where reality is whatever we say it is and all our problems can be solved with violence.

Faux Paw

NEW RULE

Don't make people who hate you hug you. Whatever the Bush administration is blackmailing John McCain with, stop.

Fashion Police

NEW RULE

Give arrested celebrities a chance to comb before their mug shots are taken! Not allowing fallen icons to wash up gives the impression that they're, well, washed up.

And we'd hate for that to happen.

Felonious Monks

NEW RULE

If you're bringing birthday cake to a chimp, bring enough for everyone. An L.A. man visiting a chimpanzee in a wildlife sanctuary was mauled by the other chimps when he didn't bring any cake for them. The man's face was partially peeled off and his nose was completely detached. And, in this town, that kind of work costs good money.

Femoirs

NEW RULE

You don't get a million dollars just for being gay. Remember Dick Cheney's daughter Mary? The one John Kerry mentioned was a lesbian and the Republicans pretended to get irate? Well, she got a million dollar advance to write her "memoirs." Memoirs? Chapter One: "My Dad's Vice President." Chapter Two: "I Like Pussy." The End.

Film Boff

NEW RULE

Let the drive-in movie die. The popcorn is always stale, the sound is always crappy, and the picture is always blurry. It's 2005—teens no longer have to drive onto a hillside and park in formation to get a hand job.

Flat Tax

NEW RULE

I don't care how big or flat it is, it's still just a TV. Congratulations—you just paid $10,000 to watch *Hogan's Heroes*.

Floral Sex

NEW RULE

"Valentine's Day Sex" is an urban legend. Every Valentine's Day ad is the same pitch: Buy her the roses and candy, and you'll get the "Valentine's Day Sex." Unfortunately, lust, over time, is just like the roses and the candy—wilting and growing stale. The last time a guy actually got sex for chocolate was when we liberated France.

Folk Off

NEW RULE

Bob Dylan must stop denying he was the voice of a generation. Bob, that's not something you get to decide. It's fate and you were it. If your generation could actually choose a voice, don't you think they'd have picked one better than yours?

Fool Recovery

NEW RULE

Former drug addicts and alcoholics have to stop saying, "I almost died." No. Cancer survivors almost died. You almost had too good a time.

For Your Reconsideration

N E W   R U L E

Take one back. Every year, along with handing out the Oscars, the Academy should take one back. Get someone up there to say, "We blew it. Roberto Benigni—give it back! We just got you out of your seat that year because we wanted to see you dry-hump Judi Dench."

Ford Galaxy

NEW RULE

No SUVs in space. The new space plane isn't a triumph of the spirit, it's a low-orbit midlife crisis. Space tourism is God's way of telling you you're not spending enough on lap dances, baccarat, and cocaine.

Forget Paris

NEW RULE

Talentless teenagers who exist to amuse us must keep up in the battle to be the dippiest twit. First Paris Hilton's topless cell phone pictures ended up on the Internet; isn't it about time Britney Spears did something trashy? Come on, honey, use your imagination. I don't know—let the wind blow your pants off, or have a miscarriage in a liquor store, or get a de-vorce from Butthead. The ball's in your trailer court.

Fossett Drip

NEW RULE

The next time Steve Fossett tries to fly something around the world, shoot him down. First it was a balloon. Then it was a plane. Next he'll try to do it strapped to a giant kite. Steve, we get it. You don't like spending time with your wife. But getting caught in the jet stream is not an accomplishment. It's just what clouds do. You want to spend your millions on a worthless cause, try donating it to the Democrats.

Fox Populi

NEW RULE

It's not a town hall meeting if you only invite people who promise to kiss your ass. Recently, three people at a Bush "social security town hall" were thrown out because organizers didn't like the bumper sticker on their car. This isn't good for America, and it's not even good for Bush. If all he wants to do is talk to someone who agrees with him on everything, he should go back and re-debate Kerry.

French Whine

NEW RULE

No more bitching about the French. At least they're standing up to the Bush administration, which is more than I can say for the Democrats. And it doesn't make me un-American to say I'd rather live in Paris than in some place where cheese only comes in individually wrapped slices.

Fresh Seamen

NEW RULE

England doesn't have to go out of its way to get gays in its navy. The British Navy is planning a special recruiting drive, including ads in gay men's magazines. *A-hoooy.* You're the British Navy. If you were any gayer, you'd be the White House press corps.

Friends to the End

NEW RULE

The end of *Friends* is not a national tragedy. It is just a sitcom that went off
the air. One week Darren was complaining to Samantha about Larry Tate,
the next week he wasn't. And nobody cared. Each character on *Friends* has
fucked every other character in every possible combination, including that
monkey. Let it go already.

California Hatin'

NEW RULE

Lay off California. The rest of America loves to laugh at crazy California, but let's remember this: California has a lot of people. And the reason it does is that lots of people from other states end up saying, "Fuck this, I'm outta here," and then they come here, where people ask them, "Don't you miss the winters?" No, strangely enough, I don't, just like I don't miss a car door slamming on my hand.

Make fun of California, but if it weren't for California, East Coast rappers would have to shoot musicians from Branson. If it weren't for California, there'd be almost no TV, and you'd have to go home at night and actually talk to your family.

The rest of America feels about California the way the rest of the world feels about America. They hate us because we do what we want to do. Just the way people think Americans are too blessed and too free, and it makes them nuts in the dreary hovels of Kabul and Tikrit and Lubbock, Texas. They pray to their threadbare gods that we'll get what we deserve, but it won't happen because we'll always keep you guessing.

We elected Ronald Reagan and Jerry Brown. We're home to Disney and also to *Hustler. The Partridge Family* and the Manson Family. We can drink a Mudslide and a Sex on the Beach during an actual mudslide while having sex on the beach. Our farms feed the world and Calista Flockhart lives here.

We have bears and great white sharks and even our washed-up actors are allowed to kill one blonde chick. We invented surfing and cyberporn and LSD and the boob job. And if we didn't, we would have.

We have oranges. Free oranges. Everywhere. What grows on the trees in Scranton?

We have a real hockey team named after a hockey team in a movie. We give our illegal aliens driver's licenses. We have a governor who digs group sex.

Would anywhere else in America trade places with L.A. or San Francisco in a piss-soaked New York minute? You bet they would, because I don't re-call anyone writing a song called "I Wish They All Could Be Rhode Island Girls."

BILL MAHER

NEW RULES

Gas Bags

NEW RULE

The big oil companies must stop running ads telling us how much they're doing for the environment. We get it: You rape the earth, but you cuddle afterward. It's insulting—like a serial killer dumping a body by the roadside and then adopting a highway. If you folks at Shell really are serious about cleaning something up, start with your restrooms.

Gay-per-View

NEW RULE

The Bravo network has to come out of the closet. First it was *Boy Meets Boy*, then *Queer Eye for the Straight Guy*, and now their newest offering: *Manhunt*, where male models skydive in their underwear. Hey, one sign your network may be gay is when it's literally raining men. One guy actually tried to score with another in midair—but his chute wouldn't open.

Gaydar Aid

NEW RULE

No more studies trying to prove that homosexuality is genetic. This week Swedish sex researchers—and honestly, are there any other kind?—found that when exposed to male pheromones, a gay man's brain reacts differently than a straight man's. Hmm. And all this time I thought my aversion to fisting and rim-jobs came from a persuasive essay in *The New Republic*. Of course it's genetic. The only people left who don't think you're born gay are Pat Robertson and Anne Heche. Can we just leave the raving lunatics behind so we can catch up to the Europeans already?

Getting Blown

NEW RULE

Don't live close to the sea. If you build your home in a place where weather knocks houses over, weather will knock your house over. People who live in the Land of Oz have houses drop on them all the time. You don't see them marching into Emerald City demanding a handout, do you? I'm sorry a big wind came and blew everything away but the La-Z-Boy and the orange velvet pool table, but hurricanes are God's way of saying, "Get off my property!"

Gin Dummy

NEW RULE

Anyone elected mayor of a place called Sin City is allowed to be a drunk. Las Vegas mayor Oscar Goodman is taking flak for telling schoolchildren that he doesn't have a drinking problem because, quote, "I love to drink," then adding that if he had to pick anything to be stranded with on a desert island, he would bring his favorite scotch. Kids, personally I would bring Eve. Because you know that freak is packing weed.

Giving Good Headlines

NEW RULE

Using the phrase "He's ba-a-a-a-ck" is over. He's ba-ack, she's ba-ack, it's ba-ack—all over. Attention people who write mini headlines for cable news: Next time you have to write one referring to Deep Throat, the swallows of Capistrano, or some rock star's hepatitis C, spend an extra 30 seconds coming up with something original like, "Hey, does it take a spike through the heart to kill off Al Gore, this grotesque freak of nature?"

Glutton, Honey

NEW RULE

Sumo wrestling isn't a sport, it's an eating disorder. You can't call yourself an athlete if your idea of getting into shape is tripling in size. Except in baseball.

Gone Fission

NEW RULE

Sometimes "sorry" just doesn't cut it. Pakistan says it's really, really sorry for selling nuclear secrets to anyone with cash and/or a thing for Allah. That's nice. When one of their customers turns Washington into a debris field, it'll be comforting to know Islamabad feels Islama-terrible. I know putting loose nukes in play isn't a serious Muslim offense, like letting women wear pants, but here in the land of the Great Satan, it's the second most horrifying thing we can imagine.

Got MILF?

NEW RULE

You can't call your show *Wife Swap* unless the other guy really gets to bang your wife. I didn't sign up for an hour of watching Mom do some other family's laundry.

Grandma Poses

NEW RULE

Posing nude is for people who look good naked, period—not for people who look good naked *for their age*. There's a *Playboy* edition you don't wanna miss: "Girls of the AARP." One sign you may not be pinup material—if you yourself have centerfolds.

Gun Fighters

NEW RULE

Know your enemies. The National Rifle Association posted a list of antigun organizations on its Web site so NRA members would know who's against the NRA. The list includes: the Ambulatory *Pediatric* Association, the American *Medical* Association, the American Association of *Surgery*, the American *Trauma* Society, the American Academy of *Child Psychiatry*, the *Children's* Defense Fund, the Congress of Neurological Surgeons, the National Association of *School Psychologists*.

Hmm. What could all these organizations have in common? Oh yeah! *They're sick of cleaning up after the NRA!*

Gyro Worship

NEW RULE

Rejected *American Idol* contestant Constantine Maroulis must be destroyed. He kept coming on to me through my television set. I don't know why you singled me out, Constantine Maroulis, but I didn't fall for it. Sure, you may have the smoky, sexy voice of a rock-and-roll bad boy, the lean stature of a Greek god, and a sultry gaze that makes my loins stir, *but that doesn't make me gay*. Call me.

Panned Parenthood

NEW RULE

Parents have to stop coddling their children. I've heard that now some schools have stopped grading papers with red ink because of complaints that a big, mean red X is too negative—why, a kid might even think he got that question wrong. Parents today are so fixated on protection, it's amazing they ever got pregnant in the first place.

A recent reality show called *Supernanny* placed an old-school, discipline-wielding nanny into a family where the mother can't figure out that the reason she's having a nervous breakdown is that she says things to her kids like, "Tyler, Mommy would really appreciate it if you didn't throw rocks at me."

Moms and dads these days are like the Democratic Party: lame, spineless, and not holding up their end of the equation. And kids are like the Republicans: drunk with power and out of control.

Maybe that's why there's also a new phenomenon called parent coaching, a kind of tech-support service for clueless parents when their 3-year-old goes haywire. As described in a recent *New York Times* article, here are some of the questions a typical mom asks her parenting coach: What should she do when Skylar won't do his chores? Should there be limits on how he spends his allowance? Should Forrest get dessert if he does not eat a healthy dinner?

Now, for those of you who are saying, "But Bill, you're not a parent," I say true, but I have one thing these parents apparently don't: a brain. This is not rocket science. What should you do when Skylar won't do his chores? How about using your size advantage? Make him!

Because if there's one thing we know about kids, it's that if you give them an inch, the authorities will raid your Neverland Ranch. Like Michael Jackson, parents these days act like they're on a date with their children—trying to impress them, trying to buy their love, and never contradicting them or giving them a big red X when they're wrong.

So no, I don't have kids, and you know what? I don't intend to have any until people start making some I'd want my kids to play with. Until then, I'm just glad I own a lot of stock in Ritalin.

BILL MAHER

NEW RULES

Hair Apparent

NEW RULE

Dye your moustache to match your toupee. You're the new U.S. ambassador to the UN, not manager of the month at Baskin-Robbins.

Hajj-Podge

NEW RULE

Update the Hajj. Every year, the words "Islamic" and "stampede" seem to appear in the same sentence when millions of Muslims descend upon Mecca to observe what's called the Hajj. I don't understand Arabs: You've got most of the oil in the world, and your religion involves walking? Next year, I want to see a looser Hajj with a cooler name, like Allahpalooza.

Hallowed Grounds

NEW RULE

Stop telling me not to talk to you until you've had your coffee, you pathetic junkie. In fact, I'll make a deal with you: I won't talk to you *before* you've had your coffee if you won't talk to me *after* you've had your coffee.

Handicrapped

NEW RULE

If you're blind, you don't have to pick up your guide dog's poop. In California, a blind couple went to court over complaints that they didn't. You see, they would have, but they can't see shit!

Have It Yahweh

NEW RULE

God is a waffler. Pat Robertson said God told him that Iraq would be a bloody disaster. But the same God told George Bush it wouldn't, which so surprised Robertson, he almost dropped the pennies he was stealing off a dead woman's eyes. But why is God talking out of two sides of his mouth? Flip-flop. God told us to beat our swords into plowshares. God: Wrong on defense, wrong for America.

Heir Head

NEW RULE

You can't be famous for nothing. Paris Hilton can't be in the papers anymore unless she kills someone, marries J.Lo, or OD's. Also, her head is too small and she only has one facial expression.

I know that's not a rule, but someone has to say it.

AND NEW RULE

If most of the pictures on your camera phone are of yourself, you need to develop some outside interests. Someone hacked into Paris Hilton's cell phone and discovered that all of her pictures are of herself. It's almost like she's an idiot. That kind of self-love isn't healthy. Lindsey Lohan loves booze, but even she occasionally buys a round for the house.

Hin-Don't

NEW RULE

McDonald's and yoga don't mix. McDonald's has a new ad that features a sinewy woman in yoga poses. And you can tell she's just eaten McDonald's because after she gets in the lotus position, she farts. Stop trying to convince me you're not the place that almost killed Morgan Spurlock. If I want to eat healthy, I'll go to a place that serves actual food.

Suture Self

NEW RULE

Stop saying that blue state people are "out of touch" with the values and morals of the red states. I'm not out of touch with them; I just don't share them. In fact—and I know this is about 140 years late—but to the southern states I would say, upon further consideration, you can go. I know that's what you always wanted, and we've reconsidered, so go ahead. And take Texas with you. You know what they say: If at first you don't secede, try, try again. Give my regards to President Charlie Daniels.

Sorry, I almost forgot—we're in a time of healing. The time when blue states and red states come together because we have so much to offer each other. Spice Rack? Meet Gun Rack. Picky about Bottled Water? Say hello to Drinks from a Garden Hose. Bought an Antique Nightstand at an Estate Sale? Meet Uses a Giant Wooden Spool He Stole from the Phone Company as a Coffee Table.

Sorry, there I go again—kidding, when I should be healing. But sometimes I just don't understand this country. I don't get that your air is poison and your job is gone and your son is scattered all over a desert you can't find on a map, but what really matters is boys kissing.

Say what you will about the Republicans, they do stand for something. Okay, it's Armageddon, but it's something. Democrats, on the other hand, have been coasting for years on Tom Daschle's charisma, but that's just not enough anymore.

Historical Blindness

NEW RULE

Not everything is a conspiracy. Black History Month is in February because Abraham Lincoln and Frederick Douglass were born in February, not because it's the shortest month. Here's the deal: You accept this on faith, and we'll pretend you didn't completely make up Kwanzaa.

Democrats will never win another election in America if they keep trying to siphon off votes from the Republicans. They'll only win by creating a lot more Democrats, and you don't do that by trying to leach on to issues that you should be denouncing. You wind up in a goose-hunting outfit a week before the election, trying to appeal to guys who would sooner vote for the goose.

These folks aren't undecideds; they're not in play. No, what the Democrats need are fresh, new ideas that are stupid, base, and hateful enough to win voters over. I dunno, like: no drinking on Christmas. Or a constitutional amendment protecting the song "God Bless America." The death penalty for missing Mother's Day. Let's put a fetus on the dollar bill—with Reagan! You know what country has been asking for an ass kicking in the worst way? Wales.

Yes, Democrats need a really, really, really stupid, meaningless, and utterly symbolic issue. And by "issue," of course, I mean "thing to hate." How about this: an amendment that says people with fish don't have the right to call themselves pet owners. Pet owning will be legally interpreted only as owning a cat or a dog. My opponent may disagree, but that's because he's a fag.

So, Democrats and Liberals, stop saying you're going to move out of the country because Bush won. Real Liberals should be *pledging to stay* because Bush won. Trust me, you can't get away from Bush by moving to France—that's where we're invading next.

Holy Matrimony

NEW RULE

Priests should be allowed to marry. What better way to ensure celibacy?

Holy Spirit

NEW RULE

The government doesn't have time to worry about cheerleaders. The Texas senate just passed a law against "overtly sexual" cheerleading. This is a horrible law. For one thing, how do these people think we train our next generation of strippers? I'm sorry, but the only time anyone in government should be spending time on cheerleaders is when his wife is away and he's actually on a cheerleader.

Home Chopping Network

Beheading hostages has jumped the shark. Come on, guys, you've seen one blurry home video of a guy in an orange jumpsuit begging for his life, you've seen them all. You've got to come up with a new twist, like one of the hostages is gay but the others don't know it, or the hostages compete for immunity . . . something. By the same token, Donald Trump has to start firing people by sawing off their heads.

Homicidal Namiacs

NEW RULE

No more serial killers with initials for nicknames, like the "bind, torture, kill" killer, BTK. It'll just encourage copycats, like "BLT," who kills you and then has a nice sandwich. Or "KFC," who kills you and then places your body parts in a bucket. Or "ADD," who starts killing you but then loses interest. Or "LBJ," who kills you while holding you up by the ears. Or RSVP, who plans to kill you, but then calls and says he can't make it . . .

Hooked on Ebonics

NEW RULE

Cut the shnizzle. We all know it's hilarious when white people—especially old ladies—talk "street" on TV, but early reports indicate that every single network sitcom this season will feature at least one 8-year-old kid saying "shnizzle." Attention all real rappers—you have guns for a reason. Use them.

Hysterical Blandness

NEW RULE

Don't type "lol" unless you really "laugh out loud." Many Web chatters have picked up the annoying habit of typing "lol" after just about everything you say. "How are you?" "lol" "The pope died." "lol" "I slowly peel back the waistband of my cotton-white briefs, unleashing my fully erect 9-inch pole." "lol" Look, if I wanted a kiss-ass session where every thought I utter gets a big, phony laugh, I'd call a meeting with my writers.

Flee Circus

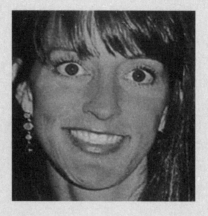

NEW RULE

Don't say a woman is crazy just because she runs away from her wedding. She'd be crazy if she wanted to spend the rest of her life servicing this goober.

When I heard the news that a young bride-to-be had gone missing on a jog days before her wedding, I had the same thought everyone else did: Man, that Scott Peterson is *good*.

Americans reacted to the so-called runaway bride by branding her as crazy for skipping town rather than marrying a Sunday school teacher in Duluth, Georgia. Ah, yes, the good life—the bake sales, the prayer meetings, the abortion protests—who could just walk away from all that? How come when the girl from *Titanic* ditches her fiancé, it's the greatest romance of all time, but when Jennifer Wilbanks does it, she's a criminal loon with a case of temporary insanity? Temporary sanity is more like it. She was staring down the barrel of 14 bridesmaids and 600 guests in the Georgia heat watching a Baptist in a blue suit sanctify her sex life with Welch's Grape Juice and a reading from *The Purpose Driven Life*—suddenly Greyhound to Vegas looked pretty good.

Jennifer, I applaud your rugged individualism. You eloped with yourself. And to Vegas, baby—that's money. I mean, what happens in Vegas stays in Vegas, whereas the woman who marries in Georgia . . . stays in Georgia.

Jen, you're a free spirit, I can tell. Something inside you snapped and rebelled at the idea of living in a persistent vegetative state—which is why tonight I'd like to offer you an open invitation to come out here. We'll even send you the $118 dollar bus ticket—first class, right behind the driver.

Come on! Come all the way over to the dark side. You can stay in my hot tub till you get back on your feet. You're crazy and you don't care about anyone's feelings but your own—you belong in Hollywood. You're a reality show waiting to happen. Plus there are a lot of eligible bachelors here. Pat O'Brien's available. I can introduce you. And I've got some stuff that you can smoke that might alleviate some of that pressure behind your eyeballs. And don't worry about that fiancé of yours. Believe me, by the time I'm finished with you, he won't want you back.

BILL MAHER

NEW RULES

I Do-Wop

NEW RULE

There's nothing wrong with being a little old bald guy and marrying a 23-year-old. That's why God created money. Stop talking about how embarrassing Billy Joel's marriage is. Driving into every tree in East Hampton? That's embarrassing. "We Didn't Start the Fire"? *Embarrassing.* This is the first thing he's done since "The Stranger" that makes perfect sense.

I Hear Dead People

NEW RULE

If you find a new record from anyone dead, it sucks. If Elvis or Tupac or Kurt Cobain thought they had a hit, they would have released it back when it could have helped them get blown.

Chicken Hawk Down

NEW RULE

The people in America who were most in favor of the Iraq war must go there and fight it. The army missed its recruiting goal by 42 percent a few months ago—more people joined the Michael Jackson Fan Club. We've done picked all the low-lying Lynndie England fruit, and now we need warm bodies. We need warm bodies like Paula Abdul needs . . . warm bodies.

A Baptist Minister in North Carolina told nine members of his congregation that unless they renounced their 2004 vote for John Kerry, they had to leave his church. Well—if we're *that* certain these days that George Bush is always *that* right about everything, then going to Iraq to fulfill the glorious leader's vision would seem the least one could do.

Hey, if it makes it any easier, just think of it as a reality show. *Fear Factor: Shitting Your Pants Edition. Survivor: Sunni Triangle.* Or maybe a video game: Grand Theft Allah.

I know, you're thinking, "But Bill, I already do my part with the 'Support Our Troops' magnet I have on my Chevy Tahoe—how much more can one man give?"

Here's an intriguing economic indicator: It's been over a year since they graduated, but neither of the Bush twins has been able to find work. Why don't they sign up for Iraq duty? Do they hate America or just freedom in general?

I Promise I'll Be Yentl

NEW RULE

Jewish people have to start having sex. The Jewish population in America dropped 5 percent in the last decade, which may explain why this country's finances have gone to shit. Breed, you sons of Abraham—breed! We need you. Israel needs you. Kobe Bryant, Robert Blake, and Phil Spector need you. Plus, without Jews, who's going to write all those sitcoms about blacks and Hispanics?

That goes for everybody who helped sell this war—you gotta go first. Brooks and Dunn? Drop your cocks and grab your socks. Ann Coulter: Darling, trust me, you will love the army. You think *you* make up stuff? Curt Schilling? Bye-bye. You ended the curse on Boston? Good. Let's try your luck on Fallujah. Oh, and that Republican Baldwin brother has to go, too, so that Ted Nugent has someone to frag.

But mostly, we have to send Mr. and Mrs. Britney Spears, because Britney once said: " . . . we should trust our president in every decision that he makes, and we should just support that and be faithful in what happens."

Somebody has to die for that. Hell, Britney's already knocked up, so that'll save the guards at Abu Ghraib about 10 minutes. And think of the spiritual lift it will provide to troops and civilians alike when actual combat smacks the smirk off of Kevin Federline's face and fills his low-hanging trousers with duty.

In summation, you can't advocate for something you wouldn't do yourself. For example, I'm for fuel efficiency, which is why I drive a hybrid car and always take an electric private plane. I'm for legalizing marijuana, so I smoke a ton of it. And I'm for gay marriage, which is why—oh well, you get the point.

Inky Dinky Don't

NEW RULE

Just because your tattoo has Chinese characters in it, it doesn't make you spiritual. It's right above the crack of your ass and it translates to "Beef with Broccoli." The last time you did anything spiritual, you were praying to God you weren't pregnant.

Inside the Actors' Ego

Stop calling acting a "craft." What witches do is a craft. Those wallets that head-injury patients make are a craft. What you do is make us believe what isn't so. You're, you're . . . a two-faced liar. And if you're going to hand out awards for that, why snub the masters?

Internet Virus

NEW RULE

You can't notify people by e-mail that you've given them chlamydia. The San Francisco Health Department has a new service that lets you send an Internet greeting card to someone you may have infected with an STD: "Roses are red, orchids are gray, congratulations, you have hepatitis A."

It's Dead, Jim

NEW RULE

Let TV shows die a natural death. Fans of the cancelled TV series *Star Trek: Enterprise* are trying to raise enough money on their own to pay for another season. It's either that or go outside. So far they've raised $3 million, largely by not dating. Hey, Trekkies, if you really want to donate money to a lost cause, try MoveOn.org.

Sin-a-Plex

NEW RULE

There's no such thing as Hollywood values. In honor of the Oscars, let me just say that every time I see some pundit say Hollywood is out of touch, I just want to take my big screen plasma TV, march it right down to the end of my private road, and throw it over the big iron gate!

"Hollywood versus America" is a tactic that works well as conservative red meat, a continuation of the "Red State vs. Blue State" theme of the last election, where blue staters were convinced everything between New York and L.A. was one giant forest where Ned Beatty is constantly being sodomized by hillbillies, and red staters were told that people like me spend all our time performing abortions and figuring out new ways to desecrate the flag. Please, they're just hobbies.

Politically, it's always been advantageous to divide people—to make America a place of warmongers versus wimps, elitists versus morons, gun nuts versus people with normal-size penises. Only problem is, it's not true. Hollywood isn't your cesspool, America; it's your mirror. We made all those movies with the smirking sex and the mindless violence and the superheroes beating the shit out of zombies because that's what you wanted.

It's what the whole world wants. Movies are the one thing about America the rest of the world still actually likes—America's last export. I mean besides the torture. And even the ones being tortured are like, "Cool, this is just like in *The Deer Hunter*."

So to those who think that if we just put *Leave It to Beaver* back on, the gay people would come to their senses, I say this: Stop worrying. Hollywood won't turn your daughter into a nymphomaniac or get her hooked on drugs. I will. And she'll still be better for it—because I'll teach her that there's more to values than reciting things, praying, and voting for Bush, that being moral actually involves making choices guided by principles like fairness and tolerance.

For example, there was a woman in Alaska who cut off her husband's penis and flushed it down the toilet. Based on that, I would agree, our morality is in decline, because 10 years ago, when Lorena Bobbitt cut off her husband's penis, she didn't flush it down the toilet, where it *could* never be retrieved. She threw it out the window of a moving car, where it could be retrieved and was. So, come on, America, admit it: When it comes to Hollywood, you love us, you really love us!

BILL MAHER

NEW RULES

Jersey, Sure

NEW RULE

Let the Mafia protect New Jersey. Terror experts say that the deadliest, most vulnerable 2 miles in America is the unguarded chemical corridor in New Jersey that gave the state its reputation for smelling like a sweat sock. Arizona has the Minute Men; let New Jersey have the Mafia. They all live there anyway.

Jet Blew

NEW RULE

After the plane lands, airlines must stop saying, "Thank you for choosing us." There is no choosing anymore. I took the only flight that left within 8 hours of when I wanted to go, by the only airline that went there. Nobody chooses Southwest—Southwest chooses you. If I need to be in Spokane, Washington, by tomorrow morning, I either take the flight I'm given, or I mail myself in a Fed-Ex box.

Ji-Hard

NEW RULE

If we really want to stop terrorism, we have to get Muslim men laid. Five British Muslims who were recently sent home from our prison at Guantanamo accused their American captors of bringing in prostitutes to taunt them. It turned out that most of them had never even seen a woman naked before. This naturally made me wonder how many members of al-Qaeda have ever even dated a girl and what would happen if we hired women to infiltrate al-Qaeda cells and have sex with them.

I'll bet you things would change quickly after this covert operation. Because young Muslim men don't really hate America—they're jealous of America. We have rap videos, the Hilton sisters, and magazines with titles like *Barely Legal*. You know what's barely legal in Afghanistan? *Everything*.

Young men need sex, and if they don't get it for months on end, they wind up cursing the day they ever decided to go to Cornell.

Have you ever wondered why the word from the "Arab street" is so angry? It's because it's a bunch of guys standing in the street! Which is what guys do when they don't have girlfriends; when they're not allowed to even talk to a girl. Of course they want to commit suicide—unlike in this country, where it's the married guys who wanna kill themselves.

But here, there's always hope that if you can at least talk to a girl, she might be crazy enough to go for you. Or you could get rich and buy one, like people do in Beverly Hills.

The connection between no sex and anger is real. It's why prizefighters stay celibate when they're in training: so that on fight night, they're pissed off and ready to kill. It's why football players don't have sex after Wednesday. And, conversely, it's why Bill Clinton never started a war.

So to paraphrase the sign in his old war room: It's the pussy, stupid. We need the Coalition of the Willing to be *really* willing. We need to mobilize two divisions of skanks, a regiment of hos, and a brigade of girls who just can't say no—all under the command of Colonel Ann Coulter, who'll be dressed in her "Ilsa, She-Wolf of the S.S." uniform.

Forget the Peace Corps; we need a Piece-of-Ass Corps. Girls, there's a cure for terrorism, and you're sitting on it.

BILL MAHER

NEW RULES

K-9 Jelly

NEW RULE

Gay marriage won't lead to dog marriage. It is not a slippery slope to rampant interspecies coupling. When women got the right to vote, it didn't lead to hamsters voting. No court has extended the equal protection clause to salmon. And for the record, all marriages are "same sex" marriages. You get married, and every night, it's the same sex.

Krystal Not

NEW RULE

Stop saying anybody or anything is like the Nazis. Republicans aren't like the Nazis. Neo-Nazis aren't even like the Nazis. Nothing is like the Nazis. Except for Wal-Mart.

Kidiots

NEW RULE

Leave the children behind. Leave them behind at least until they've learned something. A new survey finds that only half of America's high schoolers think newspapers should be allowed to publish without government approval, and almost one in five said Americans should be prohibited from expressing unpopular opinions. Lemme tell you little darlings something: This is my livelihood you're screwing with now, so learn the Bill of Rights, or you don't deserve Social Security.

Now, to those of you who think I'm overreacting here, yes, I understand that when you are in high school you are still very young and no one really cares what kids say anyway—after all, it's not like priests are dating them for their brains. But the younger generation is supposed to rage against the machine, not for it; they're supposed to question authority, not question those who question authority—and what's so frightening here is that we're seeing the beginnings of the first post 9/11 generation, kids who first became aware of the news under an "Americans need to watch what they say" administration, kids who've been told that dissent is un-American and therefore justifiably punished by fine, imprisonment, or loss of your show on ABC.

President Bush once posed the question "Is our children learning?" No, President Bush—they isn't. And so a more appropriate question might be "Is our teachers teaching?" In 4 years, you can teach a gorilla sign language— is it too much to ask that in the same amount of time, a teenager in America be taught what those crazy hippies who founded this country had in mind?

I know the Morals & Values folks want us to take time out of every school day for praying, memorizing the Ten Commandments, abstinence training, and learning at least two theories of evolution (the one agreed upon by every scientist in the world and also the one involving a naked lady and a snake)—but lest we forget, the people of Iraq risked death and danger to send us one simple, inspiring message: America, get out of our country. But also, we want the freedoms you take for granted.

I didn't mind being on the losing side of the last election, but as a loser, I guess I have some "unpopular" opinions—and, if you don't mind, I'd like to keep them. I'd even like to say them right out loud on TV, because if I just sit here every Friday night and spout Bush administration–approved talking points, that's not freedom or entertainment. It's Fox News.

Hitting below the Beltway

NEW RULE

You can't be a Washington outsider if you're already the president. Hearing President Bush constantly complain about "the politicians" and the "Washington mind-set" and saying things like "I got news for the Washington crowd" is like hearing Courtney Love bitch about junkies.

"Washington Insider" is by definition a function of one's proximity to the president. That's you, Mr. Bush. When you're given check-writing privileges by the Federal Reserve, you just might be a Washington Insider.

Put it this way: You're not the Mr. Smith in *Mr. Smith Goes to Washington*—you're the Washington part. We need a Mr. Smith to fuck with *you*! You're not on a mission you reluctantly accepted, like the old farts in *Space Cowboys*—you campaigned for it. So it's a little late to be selling yourself as some fish-out-of-water cowboy visiting the big city on assignment. You're not McCloud. For 17 of the last 24 years you've had a key to the White House. The last thing that happened in Washington without you Bushes getting a piece was Marion Barry's crack habit. *The Exorcist* happened in Georgetown, but Satan had to run it by Jim Baker first.

BILL MAHER

NEW RULES

Lassie, Stay Home

NEW RULE

No more dog shows. Prodding and grooming and training an innocent animal to fit some arbitrary human definition of perfection is abuse, plain and simple. There's only one proper way to show a dog she's adored—ask her to marry you.

Last Writes

NEW RULE

You can't write your own obituary. There's this hot new trend now: writing your own death notice before you die. It's a nice new way of saying "I may be dead, but I can still monopolize the conversation." You're dead. Worms are eating you. Let someone else talk.

Law and Order: SUV

NEW RULE

You might think this one is self-evident, but: Don't watch TV when you drive. A man is on trial for a fatal crash that happened while he was driving and watching *Road Trip*. A moving automobile isn't a theater. It's a place for eating, drinking, talking on the phone, doing your hair, checking your makeup, and getting blown.

Lemon Law

NEW RULE

I don't need an annoying little sticker on each individual piece of fruit. Let me get this straight: Our borders aren't secure, but we're still going through the plums by hand? The stickers are the opposite of appetizing—especially the ones on kiwis that say, "Don't these things kind of look like your balls?"

Let Freedom Jiggle

NEW RULE

Lap dancing is a First Amendment right. The L.A. city council has banned lap dancing. What's next—burning books? Lap dancers, or "imagineers," as I like to call them, are artists, drawing you into their fantasy world much like a skilled novelist does—that is, if novelists had perfectly waxed bikini lines. But more important, lap dancers are expressing an idea—an idea called hope: the hope that someday, a skinny young woman with artificial breasts and a navel piercing will want to have sex with you. And without that hope, millions of American men might just as well throw themselves into the sea.

Lipstick Thespians

NEW RULE

Go back to calling actresses actresses, not actors. Every word we say doesn't have to be gender neutral. And by the way, it's not a hate crime to say that Madonna is a bad actress, not a bad actor.

Lite Remark

NEW RULE

Having "no carbs" doesn't necessarily make something good. This New Rule has no carbs and it's not funny.

Lost Verizon

NEW RULE

I don't need my cell phone to play video games or access the Internet or double as a walkie-talkie—I just need it to make a phone call. Why is getting to level four of Tomb Raider no problem but to have a simple conversation I have to stand on a hilltop with my nuts wrapped in tinfoil? When it comes to cell phones, I just need the basics: something that rings at inappropriate moments, interferes with airplane safety, and gives me a brain tumor.

Love Thy Neighbor

NEW RULE

Don't try to talk to me about *Desperate Housewives*. If I had the slightest interest in other people's sex lives, I'd be a Republican.

Super Bull

NEW RULE

The Super Bowl must stop pretending it doesn't take advocacy ads. In turning down ads from certain charities like PETA, CBS and the NFL claim they don't accept advocacy ads, which is ridiculous because every Super Bowl ad is an advocacy ad, and what they mostly advocate is eating fried food and drinking beer until you explode.

Not that they care if you die from food, because death by eating is always acceptable in America. Apparently death by fucking is a different matter. There was a watch-out-for-AIDS ad during the last pregame, which is all well and good, except AIDS doesn't even place in the Top 15 of the things that kill people in this country—but what does place all over that list is food and drink: Almost twice as many Americans die from liver disease as from AIDS. Where's the Super Bowl ad with a *Will and Grace* cast member telling us to pull a condom over our Bud Light bottle?

Four times as many die of diabetes versus AIDS; 47 times as many from heart disease. We're kidding ourselves to think it's not the toxicity in our food supply that's doing us in. The nutritional guide at KFC is a card that reads "You're kidding me, right?" Guys watch the Super Bowl while eating an entire tub of guacamole and then announce, "Hey, it's the good kind of fat." No, the good kind of fat is J.Lo's ass.

And I'll have no part of the argument that McDonald's and Fritos prevent AIDS because they make you so fat, nobody wants to have sex with you. You can't even sell sex anymore without making it sound like food. How do you think they came up with "booty-licious?"

Speaking of which, you know who else is sponsoring the Super Bowl? Levitra, Viagra, and Cialis. No, those aren't three black chicks I know—okay, they are—but they're also the names of three boner pills, because let's face it: What every woman in America wants on Super Bowl Sunday evening is a gassy, flabby, face-painted drunk coming after her with a raging hard-on.

BILL MAHER

NEW RULES

M*A*S*H Note

NEW RULE

North Korea doesn't need nuclear weapons—it needs Ritalin. It's not a nuclear superpower. It's more like a 4-year-old who won't stop showing people his penis. There, we're all paying attention to you. Now put that away. Maybe the real problem is being the little brother with the hand-me-down name, *North* Korea. Why don't we change its name to something nice, like Really Really West Hawaii?

Magazine Racks

NEW RULE

Stop dressing up porn as mainstream media. The *Sports Illustrated* swimsuit issue is there to give people fodder for masturbation, which is a noble calling, but it does mean you're in the same business as *Penthouse*, *Hustler*, *Assbusters*, *Black Tail*, *Celebrititties*, *Barely Legal*, *Shaved Asian*, and the *New York Review of Cooze*.

Makeup Artist

NEW RULE

Stop saying Johnny Depp is God's gift to acting. Maybe he just likes to wear mascara.

Man Date

NEW RULE

You can't support a law against gay marriage and then hold hands with men. Being "in bed" with the Saudis is just an expression. You don't *really* have to date the guy. Although there are two upsides to getting it on with a Saudi prince: They have plenty of lubrication, and, for cleanup, there's always a towel handy.

Manual Stimulation

NEW RULE

Enough with the "For Dummies" series. The last straw was this week when I saw *NASCAR for Dummies*. Let me save you the $12.99. It's rednecks drinking beer and watching other rednecks turn left.

March Madness

NEW RULE

Let's not even try to estimate the number of people in a protest. They'll always say a million. The Park Service will say 100,000 and Fox News will say 50. Maybe it's just unknowable—like the size of space or where George Bush was in the '70s.

Mass. Hysteria

NEW RULE

Stop calling Massachusetts "Taxachusetts." It wasn't funny the first billion times. Thirty-five states have a higher tax burden than Massachusetts does. People in Montana pay more in taxes, so from now on, I'm calling Montana "Taxatana." How do you like that, Governor Judy Martz?

You and your free-spending ways disgust me. What are you, French?

Mayberry PCP

NEW RULE

Drugs are a symptom, not the problem itself. There's a reason speed is ravaging Small Town, USA: *There's nothing else to do.* Sorry, John Mellencamp, but the farms are all gone, the Tastee-Freez is closed, and the little pink house burned down in a meth lab explosion. The nearest job is 40 miles away at the Wal-Mart, and they lock you in at night. If you want the kids to stay off the crank, you need to put them on something else—a bus out of town.

Mein Furor

NEW RULE

Don't pick a German pope the day before Hitler's birthday. I'm not saying it's anything but a coincidence, but you've just given every conspiracy nut in the world a raging hard-on.

MIA Culpa

NEW RULE

If everybody was wrong about the weapons of mass destruction, then somebody has to say "my bad." When Clinton was in the White House, we investigated his business partners, his wife's business partners, the guy who was governor after him, the girls who did him, his travel agents, and the guy who cut his hair. For some reason, the two words this president just can't seem to say are "sorry" and "nuclear." Something is terribly wrong when the only person who's been fired over terrorism is me.

Mission Implausible

NEW RULE

High-profile murder suspects have to try harder. "I left my gun at the restaurant"? "I was golfing at night"? "I went fishing on Christmas Eve"? From now on, alibis for wife killing have to be at least as plausible as the argument for the Bush tax cuts.

Mob TV

NEW RULE

You don't get a TV show because Grandpa killed people. Meet the Gotti kids, Fredo, Fredo, and Fredo. Their barber is in the witness protection program.

Money for Nothing

NEW RULE

When you buy a country, get a receipt. The CPA, the American agency that ran Iraq, can't account for $9 billion it spent there. If Clinton's people had lost $9 billion, he would have been impeached underwater while sharks gnawed his legs to stumps. Can we finally stop pretending that Republicans are fiscally responsible? At least when Saddam Hussein stole the taxpayers' money, he ended up with a nice palace to show for it.

Mother Posterior

NEW RULE

If gay men can't be priests, let them be nuns. They've got the costumes. Since 1978, America has lost more than 65,000 nuns. Many left the church, but most simply died. And went to hell. Why not let gay guys fill in? The Halloween parade's loss can be the Vatican's gain.

Win One for the Groper

NEW RULE

Let the two men America really wants to see run for president run for president. Congressman Dana Rohrabacher has introduced a constitutional amendment suggesting immigrants like—oh, I don't know—Arnold Schwarzenegger be allowed to run for president. Fine, but then you have to let Democrats run Bill Clinton again. Each tribe gets its greatest warrior. Why aren't we doing that anyway?

Where is the twisted logic to the 22nd Amendment, which says you can't be president if you've done it twice? Reese Witherspoon's done two *Legally Blonde* movies—next time, does it have to be Lil' Kim?

And in a nation of immigrants, we tell immigrants they can't run? Sorry, Arnie, you can take that what-a-country, immigrant's-dream, anything's-possible crap and put it where it belongs—in a speech nominating a former town drunk from Texas.

Not to be cruel to the fine candidates who are already running for president in 2008, but why are we preventing ourselves from selecting from the top of our political gene pool? Even under general anesthesia, Clinton is more exciting than anyone else the Democrats have. A debate between Bill Clinton and Arnold Schwarzenegger? You could put that on Pay-Per-View. Hell, you could put it on the Spice Channel.

And that's the beauty of this matchup: They'd have to stick to the issues because the personal stuff would just be too devastating. The mudslinging would have to get very nuanced: "I never lied *under oath* about the asses I grabbed!" We're talking about two dudes who've smoked pot and love cigars and hummers. It would be the "you don't want to go there" election. So that's my proposal: The 22nd Amendment, for Article II, and then we can bring it on—the Terminator versus the Sperminator. Conan versus Onan. *Alien* versus *Predator*.

BILL MAHER

NEW RULES

Name Dropping

NEW RULE

Stop leaving messages on my answering machine saying "It's me." I already have a "me" in my life—me. And, frankly, if we were that close, I'd have given you the number of the phone that I answer.

Navy Seals

NEW RULE

No exploiting animals for the war effort. The military is using trained dolphins and sea lions to root out underwater mines. I remember when balancing balls on your nose got you kicked *out* of the Navy.

Newsweak

News organizations have to stop using the phrase "We go beyond the head-lines." That's your job, dummy. You don't see American Airlines saying "We land our jets on the runway!"

No Big Thing

NEW RULE

When the penis-enlargement pills you bought fail to enlarge your penis, don't file a lawsuit. Yes, I'm talking to you, Michael Coluzzi of Burlington, New Jersey. You see, Michael Coluzzi, lawsuits are in the public record and now everyone in Burlington knows you, Michael Coluzzi, have a shameful secret.

No-Coin-Do

NEW RULE

Tipping is for waiters, bathroom attendants, and lap dancers only! What is it with Starbucks, delis, even dry cleaners, all having little jars on the counter? Hmm, what's 15 percent of "blow me"? Waiters get tips because they wait on you. If your job involves standing behind a counter cutting bagels in half, you're not waiting on me—I'm waiting on you!

No Free Crunch

NEW RULE

Homeless shelters don't need gyms. Los Angeles just opened a new homeless shelter with a library, hair salon, and gym. Now, I'm fine with the library and the hair salon—like most people, I like my crack whores well read and groomed—but a gym? If you're pushing a loaded shopping cart around all day, you don't need a StairMaster. I know gay guys who became homeless just for the abs.

Nookie Monster

NEW RULE

No puppet fucking. The movie *Team America* features graphic sex scenes between marionettes. If I had any interest in wooden sex with strings attached, I'd get married.

The Crying Games

NEW RULE

One of the guy networks like ESPN has to broadcast an old-school version of the Olympics that leaves out all the "Hallmark moments" and just shows sports.

Adolf Hitler once used the Olympics to demonstrate that Aryans were strong; NBC uses them to show the world that Americans like to cry a lot. Look, I understand that everything nowadays has to be rendered bloated, syrupy, dumbed down, and sentimental—this is America, after all. But for those of you out there who may be too young to remember a time before Oprah ruined everything: In the old days when we watched the Olympics, it wasn't continuous sob-sister profiles interrupted by the occasional sporting event—it was just the events. There was none of this stuff about the heartbreak and pain it took to become the best damn kayaker a man can be. It was enough just to watch a man throw a long stick or a big iron ball. His mom's chemotherapy, his sister's glass eye, and his dog, a wounded combat vet—they never entered into it. We weren't told whose grandpa was paralyzed in a tractor accident or that the decathlon guy has a cleft palate and overcame a lifetime of bed-wetting to go for the gold, because if someone had told us that, we would have said, "Hey, if I wanted to sit through hours of melodramatic personal backstory, I'd pay attention to my date."

Take Nancy Pitts of the US women's wrestling team. Two years ago, the unthinkable happened to Nancy—she was diagnosed with prostate cancer. Happily, it was caught in time, and she was able to go back to her usual training regimen: 3 hours of weight lifting, followed by an hour of shaving.

Somehow the press now gives the Olympics the sort of coverage once reserved for a war, though actual wars are treated like sporting events. NBC aired 1,200 hours of Olympic coverage, 400 times more than they gave the Democratic convention, but what the heck, that was just about war and peace in the nuclear age—the Olympics are about swimming. Oh, if only they were! If only we could get the swimming without the three-hankie immigrant parents, the latchkey kids, the single moms, and all the brave athletes who rose before dawn and traveled hours in the frosty silence of the Iowa winter just to meet their drug dealers.

The Olympic Games are that rarest of events, a coalition of a great variety of nations coming together for a purpose other than killing Iraqis. So please, media barons, just give us one channel where it's simply about the competition and the belief that how high a man can hop is also a measure of who has the best country.

And this way you can keep the focus-group–approved drivel disguised as in-depth analysis where it belongs: in the coverage of presidential elections.

BILL MAHER

NEW RULES

Only Begotten Sony

NEW RULE

If you have to set up a big-screen TV and show the Daytona 500 to get people into your church, as one church in Fredericksburg, Virginia, does, then your flock is not worshipping Jesus; they're worshipping Dale Earnhardt Jr. And there's a difference: One is the son of god, and the other died on a cross for your sins.

Ooh la Lame

NEW RULE

Someone must stop the Cirque du Soleil. If we hate the French so much, how come we gave them Las Vegas? There are now six Cirque du Soleil–related shows on the Strip. Six! Who wants to spend 2 hours watching a bunch of French chicks fold themselves in half? You know what, scratch that. New Rule: We need more Cirque du Soleil.

Operation Dessert Storm

NEW RULE

Ice cream should stay nonpartisan. Some right-wingers started an ice cream company to counteract the lefties at Ben & Jerry's with flavors like I Hate the French Vanilla, Iraqi Road, and Smaller Govern-Mint. I know, I know, anything to get Ann Coulter to eat. But they're missing the whole point of Ben & Jerry's—hippie ice cream is fun because you eat it when you're stoned.

Osama Been Hidin'

NEW RULE

The president must stop saying that Osama Bin Laden "can run but he can't hide." Boy, can he hide. We can't find him with cruise missiles, satellites, or million-dollar bribes—although, oddly enough, he is reachable through Classmates.com.

Oscar Nod

NEW RULE

The Oscar broadcast must come in at some time under 6 hours. The Oscars are like having sex with someone on coke: It all starts out very exciting but, several hours in, you really just want them to finish.

Taint Misbehavin'

NEW RULE

Abstinence pledges make you horny. In a setback for the morals/values crowd, a new 8-year study reveals that American teenagers who take "virginity" pledges wind up with just as many STDs as the other kids do. But that's not all—taking the pledge also makes a teenage girl six times more likely to perform oral sex and four times more likely to allow anal. Which leads me to an important question: Where were these pledges when I was in high school?

Seriously, when I was a teenager, the only kids having anal intercourse were the ones who missed. My idea of lubrication was oiling my bike chain. If I had known I could have been getting porn-star sex the same year I took Algebra II simply by joining up with the Christian Right, I'd have been so down with Jesus, they would have had to pry me out of the pew.

There are a lot worse things than teenagers having sex—namely, teenagers *not* having sex. Here's something you'll never hear: "That suicide bomber blew himself up because he was having too much sex. Sex, sex, sex, nonstop. All that crazy Arab ever had was sex, and look what happened."

The theory of the puritans of the 21st century seems to be: The less kids know about sex, the better. Because people who talk about pee-pees are potty mouths. And so armed with limited knowledge and believing regular vaginal intercourse to be either immaculate or filthy dirty, these kids did with their pledge what everybody does with contracts: They found loopholes—two of them, to be exact.

Is there any greater irony than the fact that the Christian Right actually got their precious little adolescent daughters to say to their freshly scrubbed boyfriends: "Please, I want to remain pure for my wedding night, so only in the ass. Then I'll blow you." Well, at least these kids are really thinking outside the box.

BILL MAHER

NEW RULES

Pasta la Vista

NEW RULE

If you're in Iraq and you even sort of think you might be kind of near a checkpoint . . . stop. Otherwise, don't be surprised if we shoot your car. Haven't you seen a single American movie, television show, or news story from the last 60 years? That's what we do: We shoot cars. Does the name Elvis ring a bell? Richard Pryor? Lee Harvey Oswald? I know it's hard for foreigners to understand, but in America we shoot first and ask questions rarely.

Pay Ball!

NEW RULE

Stop saying that athletes do it for the love of the game. They do it for the love of their 32-room mansion with the live shark tank in the living room. Bass fishermen do it for the love of the game, which is why so few of them have agents. If pro sports paid minimum wage, Shaquille O'Neal would be a bouncer at Scores, and Anna Kournikova would be a mail-order bride from Minsk.

Pewsweek

NEW RULE

Time Magazine has to change its name to *God Weekly*. In the last few years, Time has put out: "The Secrets of the Nativity," "The God Gene," "Faith, God and the Oval Office," "The Bible and the Apocalypse," "Who Was Moses?" "What Jesus Saw," "Why Did Jesus Have to Die?" "Jesus at 2000." If Jesus gets any more free press, he's going to start thinking he's Paris Hilton. Look, I understand we have a lot of Christians in this nation, but how about a little equal time?

"Vishnu to Ganesh: 'Drop Dead!'" and "Is There No Pleasing Zeus?"

Pie-Curious

NEW RULE

Homosexuals must be ripped. As news reports covered gay couples marrying in 2004, America was forced to confront a real eye-opener: A gay person can be just as big a slob as a straight one. We saw couples with beer guts and 9-day-old stubble, wearing hockey jerseys. And I don't just mean the lesbians. Guys, I know you're new at this matrimony thing, but this is how it works: First you get married, *then* you let yourself go.

Pitt Happens

NEW RULE

Let the two best-looking people in the world have sex with each other. We all knew they'd end up together—we've been to high school. He was just waiting a respectable interval for her to shed that Billy Bob smell.

Pluck Off

NEW RULE

Ladies, leave your eyebrows alone. Here's how much men care about your eyebrows: Do you have two of them? Okay, we're done.

Pontiff-icating

NEW RULE

Don't get movie blurbs from the pope, like the pontiff's famous "It is as it was" rave for Mel Gibson's Jesus movie. What he really said was:

"James Caviezel is Christ-errific!"

"Monica Belluci puts the mmm! in Mary Magdalene!"

"She could wash my feet anytime!"

"A rock-hard 10 on the St. Peter Meter!"

Pope Goes Caviezel

NEW RULE

Stop asking Jim Caviezel religious questions. He just played Jesus in a movie. It's like asking a cast member of *Scrubs* to lance a boil. Why, if everyone on TV was really like the character he plays, no one at church would talk to me, my wife, or my eight kids.

Bi-Definition

NEW RULE

You can't claim you're the party of smaller government and then make laws about love. What business is it of the state how consenting adults choose to pair off, share expenses, and eventually stop having sex with each other?

Why does the Bush administration want a constitutional amendment about weddings? Hey, why stop at weddings—birthdays are important; let's put them in the great document. Let's make a law that gay people can have birthdays, but straight people get more cake—you know, to send the right message to kids.

Republicans are always saying we should privatize things, like schools, prison, social security—how about we privatize privacy? If the government forbids gay men from tying the knot, what's their alternative? They can't all marry Liza Minelli.

Republicans used to be the party that opposed social engineering, but now they push programs to outlaw marriage for some people and encourage it for others. If you're straight, there's a billion-five in the budget to promote marriage, but gay marriage is opposed because it threatens or mocks—or does something—to the "sanctity of marriage," as if anything you can do in Vegas drunk off your ass in front of an Elvis impersonator could be considered sacred.

Half the people who pledge eternal love are doing it because one of them is either knocked up, rich, or desperate. But, in George Bush's mind, marriage is a beautiful lifetime bond of love and sharing—kind of like what he has with the Saudis.

But at least the Right isn't hypocritical on this issue; they really believe that homosexuality is an "abomination" and a dysfunction that's "curable." They also believe that if a gay man just devotes his life to Jesus, he'll stop being gay—because that theory worked out so well with the Catholic priests.

But the greater shame in this story goes to the Democrats. They don't believe homosexuality is an abomination, and therefore their refusal to endorse gay marriage is hypocrisy. Their position doesn't come from the Bible; it's ripped right from the latest poll, which says most Americans are against gay marriage.

Well, you know what? Sometimes "most Americans" are wrong. Where's the Democrat who will stand up and go beyond the half measures of "civil union" and "hate the sin, love the sinner" and say, loud and clear, "There *is* no sin—it's *not* an abomination"?

No one can control how Cupid aims his arrows, and the ones who pretend they can usually turn out to be the biggest freaks of all.

Potty Pooper

NEW RULE

Get rid of the "baby changing station" in the men's room. Let's stop pretending that it has been, or ever will be, used. You're only tempting a short homeless man to use it as a Murphy bed.

Puck Off

NEW RULE

The National Hockey League must tell us the moment their hockey strike is settled—so we know exactly when we can all stop not caring.

Pyramid Scheme

NEW RULE

The USDA must create a food pyramid designed by someone whose brain hasn't been ravaged by malnutrition. Recently, they unveiled the official new food pyramid, in which they replaced the foods I'm supposed to eat with a color code. Judging from this, I can't tell if I'm supposed to have more broccoli or the CIA is picking up chatter in Tora Bora.

Electile Dysfunction

NEW RULE

Political conventions are important, and therefore they deserve to be broadcast and viewed in their entirety. You can't call everyone in Washington morons if you don't know exactly what it is that makes them morons.

The conventional wisdom about conventions is that they're no longer worthy of our attention because they're too "produced" and there's no "drama." You want drama? Hitch a ride home with Ted Kennedy. We're picking a president here, not the last comic standing. The media treats these conventions like pointless interruptions of their real job, which seems to be covering LA's latest celebrity murder trial. No surprises, no excitement. Hey, you know what's exciting? It's exciting when politicians get drunk with power because people aren't keeping an eye on them. No one expected we'd retaliate for 9/11 by attacking . . . Iraq! Whoo, unpredictable, exciting!

And the reason the conventions are so "produced" is because if they weren't, the networks wouldn't air them at all. To me, the sight of John Kerry rushing through his 2004 acceptance speech in a cold sweat so that he wouldn't go overtime and force viewers to miss the first 2 minutes of *Elimidate* was one of the saddest moments in the history of democracy. The man is laying out his plan for ruling the globe, and we're treating him like it's audition night at the Improv and he just got the light.

I'm not saying everyone has to pore over issues and read everything that's out there—we can't even get our president to do that. But the conventions are one of the only times when the election isn't reduced to sound bites and attack ads, when you can get to know these people a little. It's not exciting enough just to hear Teresa Heinz Kerry? Sorry, next time we'll get Justin Timberlake to whip out her tit.

Maybe the conventions aren't boring; maybe it's the people who don't participate in their own society who are boring. Once every 4 years, the two parties put on a pageant for you: "These are our faces; these are our voices; this is our vision of America's future." You'd think that would be a little more interesting than reruns of *Yes, Dear*.

BILL MAHER

NEW RULES

Racy Language

NEW RULE

Don't punish rednecks for being rednecks. NASCAR fined Dale Earnhardt
Jr. for publicly saying the words "It don't mean shit." You can't fine a redneck for that. That's not just an expression to them; it's the entire redneck
philosophy. Lost your job? It don't mean shit. Wife run off with the UPS
man? It don't mean shit. The entire rationale for a war proves to be false?
It don't mean shit. That's the beauty of the lifestyle. If rednecks had to pretend they cared about stuff, they'd be yuppies.

Ranch Dressing

N E W   R U L E

Skip the truck. President Bush is down on the ranch, and we all know what that means—lots of pictures of him in that pickup truck, as if he's going into town to pick up a bale of hay. Okay, we get it. You're a "rancher." You're "clearing brush." You're a "Washington outsider." You're a huge country fan. Unfortunately, that country is Saudi Arabia.

Rat Patrol

NEW RULE

No paying kids to tattle. A high school in Georgia says it will pay kids up to $100 to rat out friends who steal, cheat, or drink. Just like the Bible says. Because it's never too early to look into your own heart and ask yourself: What would Judas do?

Red Carpet Munching

NEW RULE

If you think the idea of Angelina Jolie sleeping with another woman is an abomination, you're gay. Normally I don't go for the idea that people who really hate gays are just closeted gays themselves, but allow me to make an exception. If you can't see the beauty in that sapphic scenario, you've got more unresolved gay issues than that dude from *Silence of the Lambs*. This is what the pope thinks of when he masturbates. It's not an abomination. It's what should be replacing baseball as our national pastime.

Reel Time

NEW RULE

Stop giving awards to movies just because they're long. It only encourages them. While I was watching *The Hours*, my popcorn actually grew into a stalk. Remember, if I wanted to be bored shitless, I'd read.

REM Job

NEW RULE

Don't try to talk to me about any dream you've had that I wasn't in. There's a very limited audience of people interested in your dreams. That's why they're only showing in your head.

Residential Library

NEW RULE

You can throw someone out of the library for how they sound but not for how they smell. A new law in San Luis Obispo says librarians can evict homeless people for their smell. Hey, lonely librarians—don't think of them as homeless; think of them as single. I know most librarians won't see much of a future with some babbling drunk with a drug habit and a messiah complex, but hey, it worked for Laura Bush.

Roidian Slip

NEW RULE

If you're surprised to find out that baseball players use steroids, we need to find out what drugs *you're* on. It was a dead giveaway when Jason Giambi gained 24 pounds in his mandible. It's time to get the performance-enhancing drugs out of baseball and back where they belong—in some octogenarian's testicles.

Row v. Wave

NEW RULE

God hates cruise ships. After years of punishing them with simple fires and plagues, he finally hit one with a tidal wave—a personal tsunami. Folks, climb off. They're filth. You could get the clap from their postcards. If cruise ships weren't damned by God and all that's holy, why would Disney own one?

Rx Shun

NEW RULE

Enough with the boner pill ads. These pills were intended to be marketed toward those with a medical necessity, not as Love Potion #9. If you have occasional trouble getting it up for the wife, try the natural method: Close your eyes and pretend she's the babysitter.

Hypocratic Growth

NEW RULE

No one has their shit together at age 22.

Yes, like many others, George Bush avoided serving in Vietnam, but the truth is, I don't really care if our president showed up for all of his National Guard jumping jacks in 1973. We all made mistakes when young and chasing a buzz—Bush blew off his calisthenics, Saddam gassed his own people, I bought the John and Yoko album where they just farted for an hour into a tape recorder.

The phrase "youthful indiscretions" is redundant because how many discreet young people do you know? The people you need to worry about are not the ones who *sowed* their wild oats but the ones who *didn't*. Michael Jackson had to wait till he was an adult to have a childhood, and I think we all see how well that turned out.

Go back far enough in any great man's life, and you will eventually get to the stuff he did or said before he was great or even a man. Don King started out life in Cleveland as a corrupt, murderous thug, but then—okay, bad example.

But the point remains: Trying to define a person's current self by their past self is the worst kind of gotcha. Our mistakes from the past are just that—mistakes, and most of the time it was necessary to make them in order to become the wiser person we then became. *You* never got drunk and pissed yourself? Or sold drugs to schoolchildren? Or panicked when you couldn't get it up at a bachelor party and killed a hooker?

Yes, if only hindsight could come without having to mess up first. And believe me, I have the platform shoes to prove that one. But to exploit youthful mistakes for political gain is—well, let's just say, when you get older, you might look back and regret it.

BILL MAHER

NEW RULES

Sabbath Schmabbath

NEW RULE

Presidents must work weekends. In 2004, the Democratic contenders for president moved a debate in South Carolina to the evening because, here in the 21st century, Orthodox candidate Joe Lieberman can't do anything on Saturday until the sun goes down. Making the schedule even tighter, the debate had to wrap up by midnight because Dick Gephardt is a werewolf.

Santa Pause

NEW RULE

No Christmas movie ads until after Halloween. Enough with this holiday creep. Give us a few more weeks of no stress before the hellish Season of Peace begins. If I wanted to hear about Jesus 365 days a year, I'd have voted for Bush.

Saving Private Cryin'

NEW RULE

Soldiers have to follow orders. In World War II, there was none of this "We're not going because we don't have the right equipment." You want equipment, join the Swiss Army. If your order is to ride a skateboard through a minefield to deliver a Zagnut bar to Donald Rumsfeld, I'm sorry, that's the deal with the army. You know what happens to soldiers who disobey direct orders? That's right—they become president of the United States.

Scary Gobblin'

NEW RULE

Halloween is child abuse. One day every year we lose our minds and send our children out into the night to talk to strangers. And then when they get home, we throw away the one healthy food item—the apple—because it might have a razor blade and keep the big sack of processed poison.

Sciatica Night Fever

NEW RULE

John Travolta must stop dancing in his movies. Sorry, John, you don't look cool anymore. You look like that creepy uncle at a wedding who's dry-humping the bridesmaids.

Shot/Ale Diplomacy

NEW RULE

Next time the Irish prime minister comes to the White House on Saint Patrick's Day, the president has to get drunk with him. I don't care if he relapses and has to find Jesus all over again. When an Irishman flies all the way across the pond on Saint Paddy's Day, the least you can do is knock back some Guinness, sing a few songs, and let him punch you in the mouth.

Sickey D's

NEW RULE

No McDonald's in hospitals. I'm not kidding—they're putting McDonald's in hospitals! Hello? You're doctors. You're not supposed to be in the "repeat business" business. I'm sorry, Fast Food Nation, but we already figured out a way to screw patients—they're called HMOs.

*69

NEW RULE

No answering the phone during sex. According to *Ad Age* magazine, 15 percent of Americans have answered their cell phone during sex. This is not only rude, it is also dangerous because it interferes with your driving. Trust me, when a woman is screaming "I'm coming, I'm coming!" she doesn't want to hear "I'm breaking up, I'm breaking up."

Skeletal Refrains

NEW RULE

In fat-ass, stomach-stapling America, stop focusing on the three people in the country who don't eat enough! There's a term for Lara Flynn Boyle's condition: It's called being a skinny chick. It's just her body type . . . as seen in this childhood photo.

Smooth Saline

NEW RULE

No, you can't have a boob job for your birthday. Record numbers of teenage girls are seeking breast-augmentation surgery—or, as they call it, "liberating a rack." Let's get back to the good old days when your daughter announced she was getting Ds—and she was talking about her report card.

So-Duh

There's no such thing as "flavored water." There's a whole aisle of this crap at the supermarket—water, but without the watery taste. Sorry, but flavored water is called a soft drink. You want flavored water? Pour some scotch over ice and let it melt. That's your flavored water.

Softening Dick

NEW RULE

Keep Dick Cheney in seclusion. I liked it better when the vice president was always tucked away in an undisclosed location. He's like the creature in the cradle at the end of *Rosemary's Baby*: It's more frightening when all we see is the rattle in its horrible little hand. Stick to your original strategy: Only bring out Dick Cheney when you're trying to make Rumsfeld seem human.

Sour Kraut

NEW RULE

"Eat me" is just an expression. Another German man has been convicted of killing and eating someone, the second such case in a year. You can always tell a German cannibal because he says things like "I'm so hungry I could eat a Horst."

Square Dunce

NEW RULE

Country music stars can't be authors. Charlie Daniels's book *Ain't No Rag: Freedom, Family, and the Flag* is a collection of musings by noted white trash icon Charlie Daniels on subjects ranging from American flags to American flag bumper stickers to what to do to a hippie if you catch him trying to burn an American flag. Before this book, I was ambivalent on the issue of flag burning. Now, I find myself reconsidering the question of book burning.

Star Bores

NEW RULE

No more referring to your acting role as "this wonderful journey." It wasn't a journey. You just mixed the wrong pills in your trailer and then went to the set and acted like someone slightly less fucked up than you.

Statue of Limitations

NEW RULE

Keep the Statue of Liberty closed. Since 9/11, the statue has been off limits for security reasons, and some people are outraged. Why? It's a sacred symbol of our principles, not a StairMaster. Everything doesn't have to be interactive. People go to church; they don't take turns up on the cross. You're not allowed to fill the Liberty Bell with nachos or wear it as a hat. You want to lose yourself inside an American icon? Have sex with Shelley Winters.

Statuette of Limitations

NEW RULE

Best sound editing is not a category at the Oscars. Ditto sound mixing. Talkies have been around for 70 years. Hollywood, you nailed the sound thing. The only part that matters about movie sound is that it's really, really loud. Otherwise, I'll be able to think, and if I think, I'll realize I'm a college-educated adult watching a movie about a Spiderman.

Stiff Up Her Lip

NEW RULE

There's no explaining love. If Charles and Camilla prove one thing, it's that she must be the greatest lay in history. She must do things to him that make Carmen Elektra look like your hand. Love is inexplicable, so let's not put any laws about marriage in our Constitution.

Storm Frontin'

NEW RULE

Hurricane names should be scary. It's bad enough we can't name hurricanes after women anymore because it's sexist; now they're all getting Waspy names like "Alex," which is the least effective approach. Can you imagine how much faster the Carolinas would evacuate if they announced that "Ludacris" was headed their way?

Orifice Politics

NEW RULE

Fucking around at the office is not a reason to lose your job. If it was, the unemployment rate in America would be 80 percent. You may have heard that the CEO of Boeing—or as it's now known, Boing!—had to step down because he was having an affair with the nice lady from accounts receivable. Who gives a damn?

I know what you're saying: "Hey Bill, that attitude may be fine for you, leading your 'single, libertarian lifestyle'—but when a 68-year-old airline executive named Harry Stonecipher bones somebody in the supply closet, what do we tell the children?"

Right, "the children," who look up to geriatric arms dealers and obviously don't want to think of their government buying Apache helicopters from a fornicator. "At Boeing, we will not tolerate sneaking around! Now get back to work on the Stealth bomber."

In other countries, a CEO committing adultery isn't even called a "scandal." It's called a "business trip." Why are there so many puritans in this country, and why can't the rest of us make them go away? When did we get to be such a nation of busybodies? Oooh, who's Harry Stonecipher fucking? I gotta know.

Just to put things into perspective, Boeing Company is our second largest defense contractor. They make things like the F-15, and we're at war, with soldiers' lives at stake, so I gotta think the smooth, uninterrupted management of the Boeing Company might be important—but apparently not more important than stopping Harry Stonecipher from grappling naked in a burlesque of lust with 52-year-old Gloria Hormth.

Not long ago, we found out there's nine billion of our dollars missing in Iraq—not misspent: lost. You heard me: $9 billion. But in the age of Bush, anything that involves money is legal, and the only scandal is sex. Gross, disgusting, AARP, early-bird-special sex with Harry Stonecipher. As if a 68-year-old man having an office romance should be a shock in the aerospace industry—it shouldn't; it should be a high five in the pharmaceutical industry. This sort of event shouldn't be condemned; it should be applauded. Harry Stonecipher's extramarital affair is the first time Boeing ever deployed an obsolete missile system and you and I didn't have to foot the bill for it.

BILL MAHER

NEW RULES

Tallowed Be Thy Name

NEW RULE

Jesus is not a candle. A company in South Dakota is selling candles with the scent of Jesus. You light one, and your friends say, "Christ, what's that smell?" It's true, the formula comes straight out of the Bible—it's from the little-known Letter of Paul to the Aromatherapists. But if Jesus really smelled so great, how come everybody was always offering to wash his feet?

Tart Reform

First Amber Frey was mad that Scott Peterson was married. Then she was mad that he had killed his wife.

NEW RULE

There's just no pleasing some people.

1040 BS

NEW RULE

That computer setup in your home where you play video golf at night and your wife has sexy cyber chats with strangers during the day is not a tax-deductible "in-home office." It's a chair in your family room, facing away from your family.

The Book of Moron

NEW RULE

If Utah gets to edit Hollywood, then Hollywood gets to edit Utah. Four Utah-based companies are taking popular movies, editing out parts they don't like, and then selling them to other sexually repressed squares. Let me ask you this, Spencer: How'd you like it if we went through the Book of Mormon and took out all the bullshit? You have your fantasy world—it involves celestial marriage and magic underpants—and we have ours: It involves Sin City and a half-naked Jessica Alba. Instead of asking yourself "What would Jesus edit?" accept that maybe *Pooty Tang* just isn't for you. You don't see me adding jokes to Pauly Shore movies. Believe me, it won't up your street cred when you bring home *Dude, Where's My Bible?*

The Guest Wing

NEW RULE

The president can have sleepovers. It turns out President Bush puts up some of his big-name donors in the Lincoln bedroom just like Clinton! And you know what? I still don't care. If Bush wants to get in his footy pajamas and have CEOs over to play Battleship, fine. If that's all Bush donors are getting for their money, it's not called "a scandal"—it's called "a good start."

The L-Word

NEW RULE

Stop saying tax-and-spend liberal. That's what the government does: It taxes and spends. As opposed to the system under Bush/Cheney: Dine-and-dash.

Three Reichs and You're Out

NEW RULE

George Bush isn't Hitler. In the 2004 election, MoveOn.org compared Bush to Hitler, ignoring the first rule for being taken seriously by grown-ups, which is: Don't call everyone you don't like "Hitler." Bush is not Hitler. For one thing, Hitler was a decorated, frontline combat veteran. Also, in the election that brought him to power in 1933, Hitler got more votes than the other candidates.

And Hitler had a mustache. So let's all take a rest from playing the Hitler card. Unless we're talking about Saddam Hussein. Now, that guy was Hitler.

Tiara Alert

NEW RULE

No more "talent competitions" at beauty pageants. Being hot *is* a talent. The only reason we endured watching Miss Texas play the xylophone in the first place was because it made her breasts jiggle. The talent contest is just an interminable delay to the whole point of the night: getting date-raped by an athlete.

Till Debt Do Us Part

NEW RULE

Enough with the bitching about the credit card companies. Sure, they're a bunch of predatory loan sharks, but your credit problems may also have something to do with the fact that you just can't stop buying stuff. So, set down your $5, double-mocha, no-foam latte and your plasma-screen, Internet-accessible, camera cell phone and face the fact that there's only one surefire way to erase credit card debt—by picking up a big, shiny pair of scissors . . . and cutting your wife in half.

Tit for Tat

NEW RULE

No breast-feeding in public. Some women think it's okay to openly breast-feed in the restaurant while I'm trying to eat. They say it's healthy and natural. Well, so is my date's libido—but you don't see her blowing me next to the dessert cart.

AND NEW RULE

You can't choose to be a cheap whore at only one specific place and time. If you show your breasts for plastic beads at Mardi Gras in New Orleans, then you have to show your breasts for beads at a Houlihan's in Philadelphia.

To Kill a Sunrise

NEW RULE

"Morning people" must keep it to themselves. By the time you stop and explain that you're a morning person, it's too late—you've already annoyed me. We get it—you're up and ready to go at the crack of dawn, just like my dick.

Tongue Twisters

NEW RULE

Lesbian kisses aren't risqué; they're desperate cries for attention. Sucking face with another chick means one of three things: Nobody is paying attention to you at the bar, no one is watching your sitcom, or no one is buying your album. Lesbian experimentation should be done in the privacy of a dorm room at Arizona State University.

Too Much Intimation

NEW RULE

If I say "How ya doin?" and I don't know you, the only proper response is "Fine." I don't need to know your mother is ill or your cat has herpes or your kid is on trial for date rape. I'm sorry you need a hug, but we're on an elevator ride, not a share-your-feelings weekend retreat. This is LA. If I wanted to know the intimate details of your life, I'd hack into your cell phone.

Toodle-Eww

NEW RULE

No more farewell tours for Cher unless it's really good-bye. Recently, Cher wrapped up her 3-year farewell tour in Hollywood. Yes, it's probably time to put the sequins and diamond-studded tiara down when the transvestites in the audience look more like you than *you* do. And if the Eagles get back together one more time, I'm going to stab them with my steely knives until I just *can* kill the beast!

Topps and Bottoms

NEW RULE

If you need to shave, and you still collect baseball cards, you're gay. If you're a kid, the cards are keepsakes of your idols. If you're a grown man, they're pictures of men.

Trial Separation

MISSING
FROM CITY CREEK CANYON
MEMORY GROVE AREA
SALT LAKE CITY UTAH - JULY 19, 2004

LORI HACKING
27 YEARS OLD - 5'3" - 115 LBS - HAZEL EYES
DARK BROWN HAIR - DARK COMPLEXION
PLEASE CONTACT SLC POLICE: (801) 799-3000
WITH ANY INFORMATION - www.findlori.com

NEW RULE

Whenever a woman is missing, arrest her husband. Who else would want her dead? She's a housewife in Salt Lake City; she didn't double-cross the Medellin cartel. Marriage is a blessed union of souls. It's also Motive One. In fact, at weddings, the preacher should just say, "I now pronounce you person-of-interest and wife."

Truck Stop

NEW RULE

Buying a car with an outdoorsy name doesn't make you Daniel Boone. Explorer, Navigator, Mountaineer, Forester—why don't we just call it what it is, a giant Ford Fuck-You-Mobile.

Crude Awakening

NEW RULE

Stop whining about gas prices. Gas costs a lot because we have to find it, bribe or kill the people who live on top of it, extract it, refine it, ship it, and pump it. You'll pay $2 a gallon and you'll like it because you know what the alternative is: riding on the bus with poor people.

How come we have cars with global positioning systems, satellite radio, and voice-activated Web access, and we still power them with the black goop that you have to suck out of the ground? Hate to tell you this, folks, but gas doesn't cost too much, it costs too little.

I know, you hear about gas prices being over $2 a gallon, and it makes you nearly choke on your $4 latte. We bitch about gas, but adjusted for inflation, it's the same price it was back when the pope was a Nazi. And it's not the fault of ExxonMobil, either. That's like Kirstie Alley saying her problem is that Arabs control all the fudge.

Anyone who's been to Europe knows that the price of gas over there is just a picture of an arm and a leg. That's because they tax it heavily, and we don't. How come we Americans accept that you can overtax cigarettes just because they are bad, but that somehow burning oil into the atmosphere is okay? You can't smoke in a bar, but you can drive through a restaurant. A little smoke from a cigar is intolerable, but a lot from a Hummer is no problem.

Of course, the Hummer is made by General Motors, the owner of other gas-guzzling fuck-you-mobiles like the Escalade and the Suburban, and they just lost a billion dollars in one quarter because it suddenly got a lot less sexy to drive one of those fake macho vehicles when it started to cost a hundred bucks to fill it up. Nobody's dick is that small.

Plus, does anybody remember the '70s? GM has been down this road before: They got filthy rich selling giant cars that suddenly people didn't want after gas prices went up. Cut to the Japanese gloating. Now they're back to gloating because they own the patent for the hybrid car. GM could have had a piece of it, but they said it didn't make "economic sense." Hey, you just lost a billion dollars in 3 months. You don't have any economic sense!

So, let me remind everyone of this: The most vulnerable point of the Earth is the atmosphere, which acts like a giant mirror, absorbing 95 percent of the sun's energy. When I heard that, I said, "Honey, that sounds important!" And I'm not even married.

If we don't protect the atmosphere, ultraviolet radiation will fry us like ants under a magnifying glass. I know these kind of facts aren't in the Bible, but maybe we should think about them anyway. After all, this could even affect Tom and Katie. It's not a real threat, like an activist judge, but it's kind of important—because, in the last half century, this precious atmosphere of ours has thinned by 40 percent. And this worries me because in the exact same time frame, my hair has thinned by 40 percent.

It worked out for me, but the Earth may not be so lucky.

BILL MAHER

NEW RULES

Unchained Malady

NEW RULE

Stop scaring us with diseases we'll never get. First it was SARS, then it was monkeypox, West Nile, and now Asian bird flu, which doesn't scare me because I'm not a sparrow in Thailand. Mysterious Asian diseases don't just come knocking on your door. Unless you're Neil Bush.

Giving Till It Hurts

NEW RULE

Terrorist organizations can't also be charities. You can't spend half your time building hospitals and schools and the other half blowing them up. For one thing, it will confuse President Bush, who won't know if you're with us, against us, or faith-based.

As the government report on 9/11 made clear—especially if you can read through a black Sharpie—claiming you're a "charitable organization" is second only to saying "religion" when you want to make people lie down and let you get away with something criminal. People like the Saudis can get away with giving money to people like Hamas by saying "Hey, they're a charity, too." Yeah, Habitat for *In*humanity.

Groups like Hamas say, "Don't judge us because, besides bombings and murder, we also provide valuable community services." Yes, and McDonald's has salads now, but that doesn't make it a health food restaurant. It's like how John Gotti's neighborhood in Queens loved him because he threw a nice block party. You can't claim you're part of the Make-A-Wish Foundation if the wish is to drive every Jew in the world into the sea. Mothers Against Drunk Driving can't also be a ring of call girls—although we've all heard the rumors.

The point is, you can't do and be everything at the same time. That's why President Bush always waits a week between wars before he proposes another tax cut for the rich. To far too many Muslims in the world, feeding children and knocking down the World Trade Center can both be considered "good works," which is also how Hamas stays in business.

But we in the rest of the world don't have to buy into this insane contradiction. If we don't take a stand now, people will come to believe Hamas really is a legitimate charity, and then we'll start getting come-ons from them in the mail, and Pam Anderson will have to start showing up at their fund-raisers with her tits hanging out. No one wants to see Joan Rivers on the red carpet with Zarqawi.

So, come on—we broke up the phone companies, can't we separate "charity" from "bad-ass murder club"? Wouldn't that be a start? And if we can accomplish that, then I predict that one day in the future, when Palestinians and Jews are living side by side in harmony, all of us sitting here today . . . will have been dead for 1,200 years.

BILL MAHER

NEW RULES

Vegetable Beef

NEW RULE

I don't care how big your pumpkin is. It doesn't reflect on anything you did. It just grew, like a brightly colored garden tumor. It's not a personal achievement; it's Bruce Vilanch in gourd form.

Vidal Tycoon

NEW RULE

Donald Trump must go even further with his hair and comb it completely over his face.

Vow Movement

NEW RULE

If gays aren't allowed to redefine marriage, then neither can right-wing Christian zealots. Arkansas has a new marriage called "covenant marriage" that requires counseling beforehand and is harder to get out of. It's a lot like regular marriage, only instead of saying "I do," you say "I double-dog swear." There's a word for couples who believe that the feelings they share now are the feelings they'll share forever: delusional. If you must enter a relationship that's bound to turn sour and is almost impossible to get out of, look into a time-share.

Hasta la Visa

NEW RULE

Only foreigners can run for president.

California Governor Arnold Schwarzenegger has stated that, when it comes to constitutional amendments, he's for one allowing foreign-born Americans to reach the highest office. At first I was puzzled by his interest in this issue, but then I discovered a little-known fact about the man: He was actually born in Austria. You'd never know it from hearing him talk, but then, he *is* a highly skilled actor.

And he makes a good point: American presidents are like American beer—bland, watered down, and advertised to us like we're morons. They come from boring places like Hope, Arkansas; Yorba Linda, California; and that ranch town where President Bush was born, New Haven, Connecticut.

Just once, I'd like America's president to be like one of those presidents Italy always has, the ones with the expensive suits and the permanent tans and the Versace mistresses, and there are photos of them making it on a boat but nobody cares because hey, *that's amore!* Quite frankly, I think of foreigners as more educated and more socially progressive, not to mention less likely to wear spurs and a giant Styrofoam cowboy hat at an international poverty conference while calling everybody they meet there "Shooter!"

Before John Kennedy, no one thought you could put a Catholic behind the desk of the Oval Office. And before Clinton, no one knew you could get a Jew under it.

Face it, the presidency is a crappy job. And who fills crappy jobs we don't want anymore better than foreigners? The average Frenchman knows more geography than we do. The average Japanese knows more math. And the average Guatemalan is already here, taking care of your kids.

The job of president is just too damn important to be left to an American. Don't we deserve a presidency infused with savoir faire and worldly so-phistication? And who better to deliver that than the grab-ass action hero from *Jingle All the Way*?

BILL MAHER

NEW RULES

Wait for the Tome

NEW RULE

No answering machine recordings over 5 seconds long. Just say "Leave your name and number," *and that's it.* Here's the deal: You spare me the endless list of "more options," the insulting instructions to "wait for the beep," and the insufferable 45-second recital from your 4-year-old, and I won't leave on your machine that I'm calling to buy more pot.

Wanna-Be Jones

NEW RULE

Spread it out a little at award shows. Norah Jones is great—we're all in "agreeance"—and she recorded a perfectly nice record for middle-aged people to screw to. But after the third award, it's just more for her maid to dust. And Sinéad O'Connor has enough chores already.

Waxing Philosophic

NEW RULE

Stop waxing your pussy. Now, I'm not talking about "regularly scheduled maintenance." I'm talking about the women who make the thing as bald as Bruce Willis's head. It's supposed to have *some* hair on it. It's a pussy, not Dr. Evil's cat.

Weakly Reader

NEW RULE

Now that the United States is 100 percent safe from terrorism, President Bush must finish reading *My Pet Goat*. Mr. President, I know you're not a big "reader," but finishing it would set a good example for the kids. It would give them a lesson in following through. Since you can't find Bin Laden, at least you'd be finishing something that was started that day.

Web Cans

NEW RULE

Don't buy other people's breast implants on the Internet. Recently, a stripper named Tawny Peaks sold her recently removed 69-HH breast implants on eBay. The secretive winning bidder was identified only as "Charlie Sheen." Suddenly, downloading songs doesn't seem so bad.

Wet Nap

NEW RULE

Sleeping with a pillow shaped like a man's arm around you, as many women in Japan are doing, is just plain creepy. If you really want to simulate the experience of sleeping with a man, press a flashlight against your ass crack.

Where Was the Honeymoon?

NEW RULE

There's no such thing as "the sanctity of marriage." The only blessed thing about this union is that VD isn't airborne. Where's the honeymoon? On a pool table? You know the marriage is a sham when the vows read, "Till Wednesday do us part."

Whore More Years

NEW RULE

Stop claiming you have an "agenda." It's not an agenda; it's a random collection of laws that your corporate donors paid you to pass. The American people aren't clamoring for a cap on medical malpractice awards. If a surgeon leaves an Altoids box in my chest cavity, I want to see him in debtor's prison.

Strip Mall

NEW RULE

Your daughter's a whore. According to the FBI, there's a new development in the prostitution game: Suburban teenage girls are now selling their white asses at the mall to make money to spend at the mall! Wow, I can't even find an *escalator* that goes down.

Oh sure, I know what you're saying: upper-middle-class Caucasian teen whoring? That's something that happens to other people's kids. But our little Ashley trading her coochie for Gucci? No way! Maybe you're right. But if your daughter comes home with scraped knees, it might not be from jumping rope. And come on, nobody buys a BMW with "babysitting money." If your kid's name is on the mall directory under "services"...

The joke here, of course, is on white America, which always feels superior to blacks and often shows it with their feet, moving out of more problematic urban areas. "White flight," it's been called. Whites feared blacks—they feared if they raised their kids around blacks, the blacks would turn their daughters into dope fiends and prostitutes. Now, through the miracle of MTV, damned if it didn't work out that way!

You see, MTV is where Snoop and Jay-Z and 50 Cent tell their stories, the stories of their youth and being poor blacks. Pimps and drug dealers were the only role models they had. And now that whole world view is all up in your kid's brain!

These days, little white boys want chocolate mamas with huge asses, and suburban girls apparently have accepted being a ho as just another hip lifestyle choice. If you take your kid to the mall this Christmas and she climbs into Santa's lap face-first, you might want to look into it. And remind your little princess, if a young woman must exchange sex for material goods, she should do it the accepted way: through the sanctity of marriage.

BILL MAHER

NEW RULES

XXX-Pression

NEW RULE

Stop interfering with the artistic expression of exotic dancers. Arizona has filed suit trying to bar strippers from simulating sex acts onstage. What else are they supposed to do up there, the Sunday *Times* crossword puzzle? They're not licking that pole because it tastes good. They're licking it because they're artists, and the pole is their canvas. Besides, once you tell strippers they can't simulate sex, it's a slippery slope to telling housewives they can't fake orgasms. And then the terrorists *have* won.

Xana-Don't

NEW RULE

Don't name your house. You're not Elvis or Charles Foster Kane or Scarlett O'Hara—you're a network exec whose crap reality show got picked up for a second season. You can name your car or your boat—call your penis "Kobe" for all I care—but when you presume that your house transcends a mere number and must have a name, it doesn't matter what you call it because people on their way over will just say, "I'm going to Asshole's."

Pique Performance

NEW RULE

Republicans need anger management training. I talk to young people all the time, and over and over again, they have the same complaint: that I'm out of Schnapps. But their other big gripe is that there's really no difference between the two parties. Not true: The Republicans are much more pissed off. Look at John Bolton—if you can. Now, I don't know if this man has human relationship issues, but I do know two things: One, his hair's not speaking to his mustache. And two, The Republicans actually like the idea of our most sensitive diplomatic post being helmed by a raging psychopath. Asking John Bolton to represent you at the UN is like asking R. Kelly to chaperone the Miss Teen USA Pageant—you know someone's gonna end up pissed.

Like Mr. Bolton, what Republicans need is to find a channel for their anger; I mean a channel besides Fox News. In the last 10 years, they've taken the White House, the Congress, the courts, and what's left of Zell Miller's mind—and it's only made them madder.

Therefore, tonight, as a solution, I would like to suggest that as a national policy, we encourage the reestablishment of the old Soviet Union. Sure, it was an evil empire, but at least it kept the Republicans *busy*! Who has time for gay marriage or activist judges or brain-dead bulimics when you've got a real bogeyman to freak out about?

The problem with American politics today is that one party has the monopoly on all the anger. To be a Republican is to walk around all day madder than Paula Abdul with a fistful of Vicodin and nothing to wash it down with. And to be a Democrat means—I dunno, your guess is as good as mine.

It seems like ever since Michael Dukakis was asked how he'd feel if his wife got raped and he said "whatever," the Democrats have been the party that speaks softly and carries Massachusetts. When Dick Cheney says "Go fuck yourself," they say "How hard?" In the last election, George Bush called John Kerry a coward, a liar, a wimp, a flip-flopper, and a war criminal, and Kerry got so incensed he almost fell off his Windsurfer. It's bad when the person in your party with the biggest balls is named Teresa.

Democrats would do well to remember this: Anger can be good. Anger can be cleansing. Anger can be a force for change. Anger is what made America what it is today—a hulking pariah whose only friends are toadies and sheiks.

BILL MAHER

NEW RULES

Yawn Jockey

NEW RULE

This year, instead of running a new Kentucky Derby, Kentucky must skip the horse abuse and just show an old one. No one will know the difference. They've been showing the same NASCAR race since 1994, and no one seems to mind.

You, Too?

NEW RULE

Bono is not a banker. Not long ago, Treasury Secretary John Snow suggested U2's Bono was on a possible short list of future presidents of the World Bank. Now, as much as Bono cares about relieving Third World debt, he should always remember that a rock star's place is in the studio or on the stage, not in a bank. Unless it's Axel Rose filling out a loan application for a used car.

Hard Cell

NEW RULE

Y ou can make fun of Lynndie England if you want, but when it comes to prisons, we're all holding the leash. America's anti-sweetheart, Private Lynndie England, has finally faced justice for her part in the Abu Ghraib prison scandal—or as Rush Limbaugh calls it, "the sleepover."

Now, a lot of people think Abu Ghraib happened because, as Americans, we're comfortable asking our horny hillbillies to fight our wars. And we are. But we're also comfortable pretending that anyone in America who winds up in prison for whatever reason somehow deserves not just loss of freedom but a brutalizing, terrifying trip to hell.

It's no mere coincidence that the guard described as the ringleader in the Iraq prison scandal, Charles Graner, worked before the war . . . where? In a prison. In America. He didn't learn to torture from the CIA or Special Ops; he picked up his abuse skills right here and took them to Iraq—outsourcing at its worst!

In a way, we are all Lynndie Englands because we know what's happening in our prisons and we clearly don't care. We tell ourselves the convenient lie that anyone who bears the label "criminal" or "terrorist" is irredeemable, subhuman psycho scum, and so whatever happens to them behind bars is justified, when the truth is that millions of nonviolent Americans have been traumatized for life in our prisons simply because they either did drugs or made a bad judgment, usually when they were young, stupid, and drunk—you'd think President Bush could relate.

There are more than two million Americans locked up, and that is not including the people who work at Wal-Mart. America, the nation that always has to be number one, *is* number one in terms of percentage of its citizens in jail: two million people total. It costs $40 billion to house this many prisoners. Do you know how many countries that had nothing to do with 9/11 we could attack for that kind of money?

In conclusion, if your response to this is "not my problem," remember this: There are monsters and animals in our prisons, yes, but most didn't go in that way, but it is how they'll come out.

Or to put it another way: If you think Martha Stewart had an attitude before . . .

BILL MAHER

NEW RULES

Zip It

NEW RULE

Don't talk to me while I'm peeing. We're not sharing a moment; we're just sharing adjacent urinals. So just stare straight ahead in awkward silence. Same goes for when we're on an elevator. And especially don't talk to me when I'm peeing on an elevator.

Muddle Ground

NEW RULE

Politics is about compromises—really stupid compromises. That's how we got such laws as: Blacks are three-fifths of a person; slaves are property, unless they make it to Ohio; interning the Japanese, but not the Germans; slaughtering the Indians, but letting the ones who survived run the keno parlors; porn, but no hardcore porn; booze, and then no booze, and then booze again. But no pot. Except medical—which is legal to possess, but *illegal* to obtain. You can't have stem cells, except the ones you already have.

In this spirit, I would like to offer a few compromise suggestions for one of the knottiest issues we face today: same-sex marriage. Why not this: It's okay to be gay if you're already gay—but no new gays. We'll grandfather you in if you're already an organ grinder, but that's it.

Or how about we let gays marry but not own homes—come out against "gay mortgage."

Or maybe the answer to this is as plain as the nose in my lap. With both sides so set—one being all for gay marriage, and the other side completely against it—how about we just let the lesbians marry? Come on, marriage is a chick thing anyway. Monogamy and marriage were invented by women and the Church as a way to address female insecurity and to stamp out oral sex as we know it. And don't give me some line about how two women can't reproduce. As long as David Crosby is alive and can swallow a Viagra, that's not a problem.

Plus, let's face it, when people talk about homosexuality being "not natural" and "an abomination," they're not talking about the women—they're talking about the men. Nobody seems to find anything abominable about Britney Spears tonguing Madonna, or Gina Gershon in bed with Jennifer Tilley, or anything else on the third shelf of my "library." But here in America, when a man puts something in another man, it had better be a bullet.

So, isn't it time both sides compromised a little on this issue: The statistics tell us that anywhere from 2 to 10 percent of people in America are gay . . . although it certainly seems higher at my bathhouse. So look, all you conservatives, I know you're sincere, and you think you're doing God's work, but in 100 years people traveling by jet pack to Mars are not going to be tripping on gay marriage. The whole issue is just gonna be a joke—on you. So my advice is simple: They're here, they're queer, get bored with it.

BILL MAHER

NEW

NEW RULES

Air Sickness

NEW RULE

Let's wait a full month before the next chick-gets-chased-around-a-plane movie. Let's pretend they already made it, and it was called *Aisle Seat* and no one saw it, and it sucked.

Celluloid Zeroes

NEW RULE

If you're going to insist on making movies based on crappy television shows, then you have to give everyone in the cineplex a remote so we can see what's playing on the other screens. The reason something was a television show in the first place is, the idea wasn't good enough to be a movie.

Du-Bye-Bye

NEW RULE

Don't have your birthday party in Dubai. Record producer Dallas Austin, who flew to Dubai for Naomi Campbell's birthday party, instead found himself in a Dubai prison, charged with possessing illegal drugs, which, in Dubai, is anything stronger than Flintstones Chewables. I feel sorry for the guy, but come on—bringing drugs into Dubai? Even Pete Doherty isn't that stupid. Listen up, 24-hour party people: Dubai may have lots of shiny hotels and Europeans in Speedos, but it's still an Arab nation, and if Habib finds the happy powder in your Louis Vuitton bag . . . well, let's just say what happens in Dubai, stays in Dubai . . . *forever.*

FEMA Impersonator

NEW RULE

The term CPT, which stands for Colored People's Time, based on the belief that blacks are often late—must now be renamed FGT, for Federal Government Time.

And when people like Mike Brown walk in anywhere even 5 minutes late, everyone must roll their eyes and mumble FGT.

H$_2$-NO

NEW RULE

There's no such thing as smart water. Hollywood starlets and models are being photographed these days holding electrolyte-enhanced water called *smart* water. Because nothing reads *smart* like Hollywood starlets and models. You know how to tell if smart water made you more intelligent? You've stopped buying it.

Instant Replea

NEW RULE

You can't chant, "America, you lose" at your trial, and then ask for another chance. Zacarias Moussaoui says he has more faith in juries now, and he wants to change his plea to not guilty. Sorry, Zac, that's not how we roll here. If we wanted to give second chances to loons who scream death threats, we'd remarry Charlie Sheen.

Reign Check

NEW RULE

The next major destructive storm must be called Hurricane George. You've earned it, buddy. Congratulations. Your presidency is officially a Category 5 disaster.

Seafood Dumbo

NEW RULE

If President Bush is going to keep visiting and revisiting New Orleans for photo ops, he must do so wearing a crawdad costume, playing the jazz trombone, and flashing his breasts every time someone throws him beads.

Semper Finally

NEW RULE

Now that they've been hit by a hurricane, the Alabama National Guard has to call up President Bush, since he never really reported for duty back then. Get out your chainsaw, Mr. President! It's brush-clearing time!

Situation Tragedy

NEW RULE

Leave *Star Trek* to the professionals. Now that there are no more *Star Trek* spin-offs on TV, desperate Trekkies have taken to filming their own episodes, complete with full-size sets, slick special effects, and their mother ruining every take by yelling, "Do you boys want to come upstairs for some soda?" Look guys, I admire your dedication, but if all you really want is to sit back and watch some elaborate, boldly-fictionalized fantasy unfold, turn on C-SPAN while some neo-con is justifying the war.

The Biggest Luger

NEW RULE

If you play a sport where most of the speed comes from gravity, you're not an athlete, you're a weight.

Truck Off

NEW RULE

There's no such thing as a light truck. Federal regulators this week proposed new fuel economy standards for light trucks effective immediately . . . in 2011. A light truck is kind of like a lite beer; it really isn't that much lighter. If they really were *light* trucks, they wouldn't have slogans such as "Like a Rock."

Trumped Terror

NEW RULE

Being black and pissed off doesn't make you a terrorist. It turns out those seven homegrown terrorists Alberto Gonzales bragged about catching in Miami didn't have any plans, any money, any contacts . . . they didn't even have a single weapon. I'm sorry, but if you're a black man in the ghetto and you don't have a gun, you're just not trying. Only the Bush Department of Justice could find the seven guys in Miami who aren't packing heat. So they had a plan to blow up the Sears Tower? Please, when I was 22, I had a plan to kidnap Loni Anderson.

Photo Credits

Page 3: Royalty-Free/CORBIS
Page 4: Top: no credit
Page 4: Bottom: Gregory Bull/AP Wide
World
Page 6: Chip East/Reuters/CORBIS
Page 8: Gary Braasch/CORBIS
Page 13: Associated Press/AP Wide World
Page 14: Bill Frausbraun/AP Wide World
Page 15: San Shi/EPA/Landov
Page 16: Top: Duomo/CORBIS
Page 16: Bottom: Lucy Nicholson/
Reuters/CORBIS
Page 17: Reuters/CORBIS
Page 18: no credit
Page 19: Chip East/Reuters/CORBIS
Page 20: Michael Germana/UPI/Landov
Page 21: Matt Brashears/POOL/AP Wide
World
Page 22: Darren Staples/Reuters/CORBIS
Page 24: William Whitehurst/CORBIS
Page 30: LWA-Stephen Welstead/CORBIS
Page 31: Ray Mickshaw/WireImage.com
Page 33: Reuters
Page 36: Reuters/CORBIS
Page 37: Courtesy of US Government
Page 38: Top: no credit
Page 38: Bottom: Mitch Mandel
Page 43: Top: Reuters/CORBIS
Page 43: Bottom: no credit
Page 44: Bill Greenblatt/UPI/Landov
Page 45: Left: Bob King/APL/
WireImage.com
Page 45: Middle: Mitchell Gerber/
CORBIS
Page 45: Right: Kevin Mazur/
WireImage.com
Page 46: Top Left: Steve Grayson/
WireImage.com
Page 46: Top Right: Jean-Paul Ausenard/
WireImage.com
Page 46: Middle: Courtesy Polly Aurit
Page 46: Bottom: Philip Gould/CORBIS
Page 47: Jim Spellman/WireImage.com
Page 51: Bito/CORBIS
Page 52: Mike Finn-Kelcey/Reuters/
Landov

Page 53: Chris Helgren/Reuters/CORBIS
Page 54: no credit
Page 55: Left: Graeme Robertson/Getty
Images
Page 55: Middle: Win McNamee/Getty
Images
Page 55: Right: Alberto Pizzoli/AFP/Getty
Images
Page 59: Steve Miller/AP Wide World
Page 60: Tim Sloan/AFP/Getty Images
Page 61: Top Left: Aiken County Police
Department/ZUMA/CORBIs
Page 61: Bottom: Handout/CORBIS
Page 61 Top Right: The California
Highway Patrol/AP Wide World
Page 62: Top: Patrick Olum/Reuters/
Landov
Page 62: Bottom: Lucas Jackson/Reuters/
CORBIS
Page 63: Najiah Feanny/CORBIS
Page 64: Royalty-Free/CORBIS
Page 65: Express Newspaper/Getty
Images
Page 66: Reuters/CORBIS
Page 67: Robert Galbraith/Reuters/
CORBIS
Page 68: Reuters/CORBIS
Page 69: Jack Guez/EPA/Landov
Page 70: Kim Sayer/CORBIS
Page 71: Top: Gregg DeGuire/
WireImage.com
Page 71: Bottom: Stuart Westmorland/
CORBIS
Page 76: Rick Wilking/Reuters/
CORBIS
Page 77: Reuters
Page 78: Top: Reuters
Page 78: Bottom: Steve Crise/CORBIS
Page 79: Ron Sachs/CORBIS
Page 80: Reuters/CORBIS
Page 81: Ray Mickshaw/WireImage.com
Page 85: Top: Yuriko Nakao/Landov
Page 85: Bottom: Reuters/CORBIS
Page 87: Left: Rufus F. Folkks/CORBIS
Page 87: Middle: Ning Chiu/ZUMA/
CORBIS

Page 87: Right: Eric Gaillard/Reuters/
  CORBIS
Page 90: Kevin Fleming/CORBIS
Page 91: Associated Press/AP Wide World
Page 92: Michael Caulfield/
  WireImage.com
Page 94: Top: Family Photo/EPA/Landov
Page 94: Bottom: Associated Press/AP
  Wide World
Page 99: Kevin Mazur/WireImage.com
Page 102: Jutta Klee/CORBIS
Page 103: David Woo/Dallas Morning
  News/CORBIS
Page 104: Albert L. Ortega/
  WireImage.com
Page 105: courtesy of Polly Aurit
Page 113: Jessica Rinaldi/Stringer/
  Reuters/CORBIS
Page 116: Eric Draper/White House/Getty
  Images
Page 119: John Stillwell/POOL/
  Reuters/CORBIS
Page 120: B. Borrell Casals; Frank Lane
  Picture Agency/CORBIS
Page 121: Gary Houlder/CORBIS
Page 122: Reuters/CORBIS
Page 127: Mike Segar/Reuters/CORBIS
Page 128: Top: Carlos Allegri/Getty
  Images
Page 128: Bottom: Reuters/CORBIS
Page 129: Gregg Newton/Reuters/
  CORBIS
Page 130: Robbie McClaran/CORBIS
Page 131: Houston Scott/CORBIS Sygma
Page 132: Max Rossi/Reuters/CORBIS
Page 133: Jay C. Clendenin/POOL/
  CORBIS
Page 134: Left: Associated Press/AP Wide
  World
Page 134: Middle: Pacha/CORBIS
Page 134: Right: Reuters/CORBIS
Page 135: Top:Kevin Mazur/
  WireImage.com
Page 135: Bottom: John Van Hasselt/
  CORBIS Sygma
Page 139: Reuters
Page 141: no credit
Page 147: Reuters/CORBIS
Page 148: Left: Jason Reed/Reuters/
  CORBIS
Page 148: Right: Reuters/CORBIS
Page 149: Gabe Palmer/CORBIS

Page 153: Ed Betz/AP Wide World
Page 154: no credit for all
Page 155: John Sciulli/WireImage.com
Page 156: George B. Diebold/CORBIS
Page 157: Philippe Antonello/EPA/
  Landov
Page 161: Courtesy of US Government
Page 165: Leo Dennis/Newsport/CORBIS
Page 166: Top: Kevin Lamarque/Reuters
Page 166: Bottom: Reuters/CORBIS
Page 167: Reuters/CORBIS
Page 174: MPI/Getty Images
Page 176: Top: Flynet Pictures Inc.
Page 176: Bottom: Nick Ut/AP Wide
  World
Page 177: Robert Galbraith/Reuters/
  CORBIS
Page 179: Alan Schein/CORBIS
Page 185: Paul Sakuma-Pool/Getty
  Images
Page 187: Eric Draper/White House/
  Handout/Reuters/CORBIS
Page 188: Top Left: Brooks Kraft/
  CORBIS
Page 188: Top Right: Bettmann/CORBIS
Page 188: Bottom: Thomas
  Hartwell/Time Life Pictures/Getty
  Images
Page 189: Reuters/CORBIS
Page 191: Kevin Kane/WireImage.com
Page 192: Reuters/CORBIS
Page 193: FindLori.com/Reuters/Landov
Page 203: Top: Royalty-Free/CORBIS
Page 203: Bottom: Frederick M. Brown/
  Newsmakers
Page 204: Reuters
Page 205: Kimberly White/Reuters/
  CORBIS
Page 209: Scott Gries/Getty Images
Page 211: Kim Kyung-Hoon/Reuters/
  Landov
Page 212: Barry King/WireImage.com
Page 213: Jason Reed/Reuters/CORBIS
Page 217: Moshe Shai/CORBIS
Page 219: Left: Seokyong Lee/Bloomberg
  News/Landov
Page 219: Middle: Tannen Maury/Landov
Page 219: Right: Shawn Thew/EPA/
  Landov
Page 223: Dan Herrick-KPA/ZUMA/
  CORBIS
Page 231: Reuters